PARADISE LOST

John Milton

EDITORIAL DIRECTOR Laurie Barnett
DIRECTOR OF TECHNOLOGY Tammy Hepps

SERIES EDITOR John Crowther
MANAGING EDITOR Vincent Janoski

WRITERS Patrick Gardner, James Sitar
EDITORS John Crowther, Emma Chastain

This edition published by Spark Publishing

Spark Publishing
A Division of SparkNotes LLC
120 Fifth Avenue, 8th Floor
New York, NY 10011

Please submit all comments and questions or report errors to www.sparknotes.com/errors

Printed and bound in the United States

ISBN 1-58663-377-5

Introduction:
Stopping to Buy SparkNotes on a Snowy Evening

Whose words these are you *think* you know.
Your paper's due tomorrow, though;
We're glad to see you stopping here
To get some help before you go.

Lost your course? You'll find it here.
Face tests and essays without fear.
Between the words, good grades at stake:
Get great results throughout the year.

Once school bells caused your heart to quake
As teachers circled each mistake.
Use SparkNotes and no longer weep,
Ace every single test you take.

Yes, books are lovely, dark, and deep,
But only what you grasp you keep,
With hours to go before you sleep,
With hours to go before you sleep.

CONTENTS

Context

Milton's Life

John Milton was born on December 9, 1608, in London. Milton's father was a prosperous merchant, despite the fact that he had been disowned by his family when he converted from Catholicism to Protestantism. Milton excelled in school, and went on to study privately in his twenties and thirties. In 1638 he made a trip to Italy, studying in Florence, Siena, and Rome, but felt obliged to return home upon the outbreak of civil war in England, in 1639. Upon his return from Italy, he began planning an epic poem, the first ever written in English. These plans were delayed by his marriage to Mary Powell and her subsequent desertion of him. In reaction to these events, Milton wrote a series of pamphlets calling for more leniency in the church's position on divorce. His argument brought him both greater publicity and angry criticism from the religious establishment in England. When the Second Civil War ended in 1648, with King Charles dethroned and executed, Milton welcomed the new parliament and wrote pamphlets in its support. After serving for a few years in a civil position, he retired briefly to his house in Westminster because his eyesight was failing. By 1652 he was completely blind.

Despite his disability, Milton reentered civil service under the protectorate of Oliver Cromwell, the military general who ruled the British Isles from 1653 to 1658. Two years after Cromwell's death, Milton's worst fears were realized—the Restoration brought Charles II back to the throne, and the poet had to go into hiding to escape execution. However, he had already begun work on the great English epic which he had planned so long before: *Paradise Lost*. Now he had the opportunity to work on it in earnest. It was published in 1667, a year after the Great Fire of London. The greatness of Milton's epic was immediately recognized, and the admiring comments of the respected poets John Dryden and Andrew Marvell helped restore Milton to favor. He spent the ensuing years at his residence in Bunhill, still writing prolifically. Milton died at home on November 8, 1674. By all accounts, Milton led a studious and quiet life from his youth up until his death.

EDUCATION

Thanks to his father's wealth, young Milton got the best education money could buy. He had a private tutor as a youngster. As a young teenager he attended the prestigious St. Paul's Cathedral School. After he excelled at St. Paul's he entered college at Christ's College at Cambridge University. At the latter, he made quite a name for himself with his prodigious writing, publishing several essays and poems to high acclaim. After graduating with his master's degree in 1632, Milton was once again accommodated by his father. He was allowed to take over the family's estate near Windsor and pursue a quiet life of study. He spent 1632 to 1638—his mid to late twenties—reading the classics in Greek and Latin and learning new theories in mathematics and music.

Milton became fluent in many foreign and classical languages, including Italian, Greek, Latin, Aramaic, Hebrew, French, Spanish, Anglo-Saxon, and spoke some Dutch as well. His knowledge of most of these languages was immense and precocious. He wrote sonnets in Italian as a teenager. While a student at Cambridge, he was invited in his second year to address the first year students in a speech written entirely in Latin.

After Cambridge, Milton continued a quiet life of study well through his twenties. By the age of thirty, Milton had made himself into one of the most brilliant minds of England, and one of the most ambitious poets it had ever produced.

EARLY WORKS

In his twenties, Milton wrote five masterful long poems, each of them influential and important in its own separate way: "On the Morning of Christ's Nativity," "Comus," "Lycidas," "Il Penseroso," and "L'Allegro." Through these poems, Milton honed his skills at writing narrative, dramatic, elegiac, philosophical, and lyrical poetry. He had built a firm poetic foundation through his intense study of languages, philosophy, and politics, and fused it with his uncanny sense of tone and diction. Even in these early poems, Milton's literary output was guided by his faith in God. Milton believed that all poetry served a social, philosophical, and religious purpose. He thought that poetry should glorify God, promote religious values, enlighten readers, and help people to become better Christians.

Aside from his poetic successes, Milton was also a prolific writer of essays and pamphlets. These prose writings did not bring Milton public acclaim. In fact, since his essays and pamphlets argued against the established views of most of England, Milton was even the object of threats. Nevertheless, he continued to form the basis for his political and theological beliefs in the form of essays and pamphlets.

POLITICS

Milton's political ideals are expressed in the many pamphlets he wrote during his lifetime. He championed the absolute freedom of the individual—perhaps because he had been so often betrayed by the institutions in which he put his trust. His distrust of institutions was accompanied by his belief that power corrupts human beings. He distrusted anyone who could claim power over anyone else, and believed that rulers should have to prove their right to lead other people.

Milton was an activist in his middle years, fighting for human rights and against the rule of England's leaders, whom he believed were inept. Knowing he was not a fighter, he demonstrated his activism by writing lengthy, rhetorical pamphlets that thoroughly and rigorously argue for his point of view. Although he championed liberty and fought against authority throughout his career, in theory he believed in a strict social and political hierarchy in which people would obey their leaders and leaders serve their people. He believed that leaders should be leaders because they are better and more fit to rule than their subjects. But despite these rigid views of authority, Milton believed that the social hierarchy that actually existed in his day was extremely corrupt, and he directly challenged the rule of Charles I, the king of England during much of Milton's lifetime. Milton argued that Charles was not, in fact, fit to lead his subjects because he did not possess superior faculties or virtues.

RELIGION

Milton took public stances on a great number of issues, but most important to the reading of *Paradise Lost* are his positions on religion. In Milton's time, the Anglican Church, or Church of England, had split into the high Anglican, moderate Anglican, and Puritan or Presbyterian sects. Milton was a Presbyterian. This denomination called for the abolishment of bishops, an office that exists as part of the Catholic and Anglican churches. Milton, however, gradually took his views further, ultimately calling for the removal of all priests, whom he referred to as "hirelings." Milton despised the corruption he saw in the Catholic Church, repeatedly attacking it both in his poetry and prose. In "Lycidas," he likens Catholics to hungry wolves leaping into a sheep's pen, an image similar to his depiction of Satan leaping over the wall of Paradise in *Paradise Lost,* Book IV. He saw few problems with the division of Protestants into more and smaller denominations. Instead, he thought that the fragmentation of churches was a sign of healthy self-examination, and believed that each individual Christian should be his own church, without any establishment to encumber him. These beliefs, expressed in a great number of pamphlets, prompted his break with the Presbyterians before 1650. From that point on, Milton advocated the complete abolishment of all church establishments, and kept his own private religion, close to the Calvinism practiced by Presbyterians but differing in some ways. Milton's highly individual view of Christianity makes *Paradise Lost* simultaneously personal and universal.

In his later years, Milton came to view all organized Christian churches, whether Anglican, Catholic or Presbyterian, as an obstacle to true faith. He felt that the individual and his conscience (or "right reason") was a much more powerful tool in interpreting the Word of God than the example set by a church. Throughout Paradise Lost, Milton expresses the idea that Adam and Eve's fall from grace was actually fortunate, because it gives individual human beings the opportunity to redeem themselves by true repentance and faith. The importance of remaining strong in one's personal religious convictions, particularly in the face of widespread condemnation, is a major theme in the later *Books of Paradise Lost,* as Michael shows Adam the vision of Enoch and Noah, two followers of God who risk death to stand up for him.

Paradise Lost also presents a number of Protestant Christian positions: the union of the Old and New Testaments, the unworthiness of mankind, and the importance of Christ's love in man's salvation. Nonetheless, the poem does not present a unified, cohesive theory of Christian theology, nor does it attempt to identify disbelievers, redefine Christianity, or replace the Bible. Instead, Milton's epic stands as a remarkable presentation of biblical stories meant to engage Christian readers and help them to be better Christians.

WOMEN AND MARRIAGE

Much of Milton's social commentary in *Paradise Lost* focuses on the proper role of women. In Book IV he makes clear that he does not think men and women are equals, alluding to biblical passages that identify man as the master of woman. Although Milton viewed women as inferior to men, believing that wives should be subservient to their husbands, he did not see himself as a woman-hater. In *Paradise Lost,* he distances himself from the misogyny popular in his time—the belief that women are utterly inferior to men, essentially evil, and generally to be avoided. Milton's character Adam voices this harsh view of womankind, but only after the fall, as an expression of anger and frustration. Put simply, Milton's early views in *Paradise Lost* may be misogynistic by today's standards, but he nevertheless presents Eve's wifely role as an important one, as Adam and Eve help one another to become better and more complete individuals.

Milton's views on marriage are mainstream today, but they were viewed as shocking and heretical in his own time. Milton was a pioneer for the right of divorce in an age when divorce was prohibited by nearly all denominations. In fact, the only grounds for a lawful divorce in Milton's time was usually sexual incompatibility due to unlawful relations with other parties. But in his *Doctrine of Discipline and Divorce,* Milton expresses his belief that any sort of incompatibility—sexual, mental, or otherwise—is justified grounds for a divorce. In the same essay, he argues that the main purpose of marriage is not necessarily procreation, as most people thought at that time, but to bring two people together in completion. He felt that conversation and mental companionship were supremely important in a marriage, and admits that his first marriage might have failed due to a lack in this regard. He also argued that the partners in a marriage must complement each other. His portrayal of Adam and Eve after the fall is a vivid example of his belief that two people can complement each other, smoothing out one anothers' faults and enhancing each others' strengths.

THE EPIC

At the early age of sixteen, Milton already aspired to write the great English epic. As he read the classical epics in school—Homer's *Odyssey* and *Iliad* and Virgil's *Aeneid*—he began to fantasize about bringing such artistic brilliance to the English language.

Milton considered many topics for his epic. Early on, he thought that the story of King Arthur and the Knights of the Round Table was a noble topic. Then, as he grew slightly older, he hoped to write an epic about Oliver Cromwell, who took control of England in 1653 after helping to dethrone and execute King Charles. Judging from these two topics, it is clear that Milton wanted to write his epic on a distinctly British topic that would inspire nationalist pride in his countrymen. Such a topic would also mimic Homer's and Virgil's nationalist epics of strong, virtuous warriors and noble battles. However, Milton abandoned both of these ideas, and for a time gave up the notion of writing an epic at all.

But in the mid-1650s, Milton returned to an idea he had previously had for a verse play: the story of Adam and Eve. He concluded that the story might fail as a drama but succeed as an epic. In 1656 the blind Milton began to recite verse each morning to one of his two daughters, who wrote his poem down for him. Milton continued to dictate *Paradise Lost* for several years, finishing in 1667 when it was first published in ten books. Milton soon returned to revise his epic, redividing it into twelve books (as the classical epics were divided), and publishing it in its authoritative second edition form in 1671.

Later in 1671 he published his final work: *Paradise Regained*, the sequel to his great epic. Due to his strong religious beliefs, Milton thought that this work surpassed *Paradise Lost* in both its art and its message, though most readers today would disagree.

Plot Overview

ILTON'S SPEAKER BEGINS *Paradise Lost* by stating that his subject will be Adam and Eve's disobedience and fall from grace. He invokes a heavenly muse and asks for help in relating his ambitious story and God's plan for humankind. The action begins with Satan and his fellow rebel angels who are found chained to a lake of fire in Hell. They quickly free themselves and fly to land, where they discover minerals and construct Pandemonium, which will be their meeting place. Inside Pandemonium, the rebel angels, who are now devils, debate whether they should begin another war with God. Beezlebub suggests that they attempt to corrupt God's beloved new creation, humankind. Satan agrees, and volunteers to go himself. As he prepares to leave Hell, he is met at the gates by his children, Sin and Death, who follow him and build a bridge between Hell and Earth.

In Heaven, God orders the angels together for a council of their own. He tells them of Satan's intentions, and the Son volunteers himself to make the sacrifice for humankind. Meanwhile, Satan travels through Night and Chaos and finds Earth. He disguises himself as a cherub to get past the Archangel Uriel, who stands guard at the sun. He tells Uriel that he wishes to see and praise God's glorious creation, and Uriel assents. Satan then lands on Earth and takes a moment to reflect. Seeing the splendor of Paradise brings him pain rather than pleasure. He reaffirms his decision to make evil his good, and continue to commit crimes against God. Satan leaps over Paradise's wall, takes the form of a cormorant (a large bird), and perches himself atop the Tree of Life. Looking down at Satan from his post, Uriel notices the volatile emotions reflected in the face of this so-called cherub and warns the other angels that an impostor is in their midst. The other angels agree to search the Garden for intruders.

Meanwhile, Adam and Eve tend the Garden, carefully obeying God's supreme order not to eat from the Tree of Knowledge. After a long day of work, they return to their bower and rest. There, Satan takes the form of a toad and whispers into Eve's ear. Gabriel, the angel set to guard Paradise, finds Satan there and orders him to leave. Satan prepares to battle Gabriel, but God makes a sign appear in the sky—the golden scales of justice—and Satan scurries away.

Eve awakes and tells Adam about a dream she had, in which an angel tempted her to eat from the forbidden tree. Worried about his creation, God sends Raphael down to Earth to teach Adam and Eve of the dangers they face with Satan.

Raphael arrives on Earth and eats a meal with Adam and Eve. After the meal, Eve retires, allowing Raphael and Adam to speak alone. Raphael relates the story of Satan's envy over the Son's appointment as God's second-in-command. Satan gathered other angels together who were also angry to hear this news, and together they plotted a war against God. Abdiel decides not to join Satan's army and returns to God. The angels then begin to fight, with Michael and Gabriel serving as co-leaders for Heaven's army. The battle lasts two days, when God sends the Son to end the war and deliver Satan and his rebel angels to Hell. Raphael tells Adam about Satan's evil motives to corrupt them, and warns Adam to watch out for Satan. Adam asks Raphael to tell him the story of creation. Raphael tells Adam that God sent the Son into Chaos to create the universe. He created the earth and stars and other planets. Curious, Adam asks Raphael about the movement of the stars and planets. Raphael promptly warns Adam about his seemingly unquenchable search for knowledge. Raphael tells Adam that he will learn all he needs to know, and that any other knowledge is not meant for humans to comprehend. Adam tells Raphael about his first memories, of waking up and wondering who he was, what he was, and where he was. Adam says that God spoke to him and told him many things, including his order not to eat from the Tree of Knowledge. After the story, Adam confesses to Raphael his intense physical attraction to Eve. Raphael reminds Adam that he must love Eve more purely and spiritually. With this final bit of advice, Raphael leaves Earth and returns to Heaven.

Eight days after his banishment, Satan returns to Paradise. After closely studying the animals of Paradise, he chooses to take the form of the serpent. Meanwhile, Eve suggests to Adam that they work separately for awhile, so they can get more work done. Adam is hesitant but then assents. Satan searches for Eve and is delighted to find her alone. In the form of a serpent, he talks to Eve and compliments her on her beauty and godliness. She is amazed to find an animal that can speak. She asks how he learned to speak, and he tells her that it was by eating from the Tree of Knowledge. He tells Eve that God actually wants her and Adam to eat from the tree, and that his order is merely a test of their courage. She is hesitant at first but then reaches for a fruit from the Tree of Knowledge and eats. She becomes distraught and searches for Adam. Adam has been busy making a wreath of flowers for Eve. When Eve finds Adam, he drops the wreath and is horrified to find that Eve has eaten from the forbidden tree. Knowing that she has fallen, he decides that he would rather be fallen with her than remain pure and lose her. So he eats from the fruit as well. Adam looks at Eve in a new way, and together they turn to lust.

God immediately knows of their disobedience. He tells the angels in Heaven that Adam and Eve must be punished, but with a display of both justice and mercy. He sends the Son to give out the punishments. The Son first punishes the serpent whose body Satan took, and condemns it never to walk upright again. Then the Son tells Adam and Eve that they must now suffer pain and death. Eve and all women must suffer the pain of childbirth and must submit to their husbands, and Adam and all men must hunt and grow their own food on a depleted Earth. Meanwhile, Satan returns to Hell where he is greeted with cheers. He speaks to the devils in Pandemonium, and everyone believes that he has beaten God. Sin and Death travel the bridge they built on their way to Earth. Shortly thereafter, the devils unwillingly transform into snakes and try to reach fruit from imaginary trees that shrivel and turn to dust as they reach them.

God tells the angels to transform the Earth. After the fall, humankind must suffer hot and cold seasons instead of the consistent temperatures before the fall. On Earth, Adam and Eve fear their approaching doom. They blame each other for their disobedience and become increasingly angry at one another. In a fit of rage, Adam wonders why God ever created Eve. Eve begs Adam not to abandon her. She tells him that they can survive by loving each other. She accepts the blame because she has disobeyed both God and Adam. She ponders suicide. Adam, moved by her speech, forbids her from taking her own life. He remembers their punishment and believes that they can enact revenge on Satan by remaining obedient to God. Together they pray to God and repent.

God hears their prayers, and sends Michael down to Earth. Michael arrives on Earth, and tells them that they must leave Paradise. But before they leave, Michael puts Eve to sleep and takes Adam up onto the highest hill, where he shows him a vision of humankind's future. Adam sees the sins of his children, and his children's children, and his first vision of death. Horrified, he asks Michael if there is any alternative to death. Generations to follow continue to sin by lust, greed, envy, and pride. They kill each other selfishly and live only for pleasure. Then Michael shows him the vision of Enoch, who is saved by God as his warring peers attempt to kill him. Adam also sees the story of Noah and his family, whose virtue allows them to be chosen to survive the flood that kills all other humans. Adam feels remorse for death and happiness for humankind's redemption. Next is the vision of Nimrod and the Tower of Babel. This story explains the perversion of pure language into the many languages that are spoken on Earth today. Adam sees the triumph of Moses and the Israelites, and then glimpses the Son's sacrifice to save humankind. After this vision, it is time for Adam and Eve to leave Paradise. Eve awakes and tells Adam that she had a very interesting and educating dream. Led by Michael, Adam and Eve slowly and woefully leave Paradise hand in hand into a new world.

Character List

Main Characters

Satan   Head of the rebellious angels who have just fallen from Heaven. As the poem's antagonist, Satan is the originator of sin—the first to be ungrateful for God the Father's blessings. He embarks on a mission to Earth that even-tually leads to the fall of Adam and Eve, but also worsens his eternal punishment. His character changes through-out the poem. Satan often appears to speak rationally and persuasively, but later in the poem we see the incon-sistency and irrationality of his thoughts. He can assume any form, adopting both glorious and humble shapes.

Adam   The first human, the father of our race, and, along with his wife Eve, the caretaker of the Garden of Eden. Adam is grateful and obedient to God, but falls from grace when Eve convinces him to join her in the sin of eating from the Tree of Knowledge.

Eve   The first woman and the mother of mankind. Eve was made from a rib taken from Adam's side. Because she was made from Adam and for Adam, she is subservient to him. She is also weaker than Adam, so Satan focuses his powers of temptation on her. He succeeds in getting her to eat the fruit of the forbidden tree despite God's command.

God the Father   One part of the Christian Trinity. God the Father creates the world by means of God the Son, creating Adam and Eve last. He foresees the fall of mankind through them. He does not prevent their fall, in order to preserve their free will, but he does allow his Son to atone for their sins.

God the Son Jesus Christ, the second part of the Trinity. He delivers the fatal blow to Satan's forces, sending them down into Hell, before the creation of Earth. When the fall of man is predicted, He offers himself as a sacrifice to pay for the sins of mankind, so that God the Father can be both just and merciful.

DEVILS, INHABITING HELL

Beelzebub Satan's second-in-command. Beelzebub discusses with Satan their options after being cast into Hell, and at the debate suggests that they investigate the newly created Earth. He and Satan embody perverted reason, since they are both eloquent and rational but use their talents for wholly corrupt ends.

Belial One of the principal devils in Hell. Belial argues against further war with Heaven, but he does so because he is an embodiment of sloth and inactivity, not for any good reason. His eloquence and learning is great, and he is able to persuade many of the devils with his faulty reasoning.

Mammon A devil known in the Bible as the epitome of wealth. Mammon always walks hunched over, as if he is searching the ground for valuables. In the debate among the devils, he argues against war, seeing no profit to be gained from it. He believes Hell can be improved by mining the gems and minerals they find there.

Mulciber The devil who builds Pandemonium, Satan's palace in Hell. Mulciber's character is based on a Greek mythological figure known for being a poor architect, but in Milton's poem he is one of the most productive and skilled devils in Hell.

Moloch A rash, irrational, and murderous devil. Moloch argues in Pandemonium that the devils should engage in another full war against God and his servant angels.

Sin	Satan's daughter, who sprang full-formed from Satan's head when he was still in Heaven. Sin has the shape of a woman above the waist, that of a serpent below, and her middle is ringed about with Hell Hounds, who periodically burrow into her womb and gnaw her entrails. She guards the gates of Hell.
Death	Satan's son by his daughter, Sin. Death in turn rapes his mother, begetting the mass of beasts that torment her lower half. The relations between Death, Sin, and Satan mimic horribly those of the Holy Trinity.

ANGELS, INHABITING HEAVEN AND EARTH

Gabriel	One of the archangels of Heaven, who acts as a guard at the Garden of Eden. Gabriel battles Satan after his angels find Satan whispering to Eve in the Garden.
Raphael	One of the archangels in Heaven, who acts as one of God's messengers. Raphael informs Adam of Satan's plot to seduce them into sin, and also narrates the story of the fallen angels, as well as the fall of Satan.
Uriel	An angel who guards the planet earth. Uriel is the angel whom Satan tricks when he is disguised as a cherub. Uriel, as a good angel and guardian, tries to correct his error by making the other angels aware of Satan's presence.
Abdiel	An angel who at first considers joining Satan in rebellion but argues against Satan and the rebel angels and returns to God. His character demonstrates the power of repentance.
Michael	The chief of the archangels, Michael leads the angelic forces against Satan and his followers in the battle in Heaven, before the Son provides the decisive advantage. Michael also stands guard at the Gate of Heaven, and narrates the future of the world to Adam in Books XI and XII.

CHARACTER LIST

ANALYSIS OF MAJOR CHARACTERS

SATAN

Some readers consider Satan to be the hero, or protagonist, of the story, because he struggles to overcome his own doubts and weaknesses and accomplishes his goal of corrupting humankind. This goal, however, is evil, and Adam and Eve are the moral heroes at the end of the story, as they help to begin humankind's slow process of redemption and salvation. Satan is far from being the story's object of admiration, as most heroes are. Nor does it make sense for readers to celebrate or emulate him, as they might with a true hero. Yet there are many compelling qualities to his character that make him intriguing to readers.

One source of Satan's fascination for us is that he is an extremely complex and subtle character. It would be difficult, perhaps impossible, for Milton to make perfect, infallible characters such as God the Father, God the Son, and the angels as interesting to read about as the flawed characters, such as Satan, Adam, and Eve. Satan, moreover, strikes a grand and majestic figure, apparently unafraid of being damned eternally, and uncowed by such terrifying figures as Chaos or Death. Many readers have argued that Milton deliberately makes Satan seem heroic and appealing early in the poem to draw us into sympathizing with him against our will, so that we may see how seductive evil is and learn to be more vigilant in resisting its appeal.

Milton devotes much of the poem's early books to developing Satan's character. Satan's greatest fault is his pride. He casts himself as an innocent victim, overlooked for an important promotion. But his ability to think so selfishly in Heaven, where all angels are equal and loved and happy, is surprising. His confidence in thinking that he could ever overthrow God displays tremendous vanity and pride. When Satan shares his pain and alienation as he reaches Earth in Book IV, we may feel somewhat sympathetic to him or even identify with him. But Satan continues to devote himself to evil. Every speech he gives is fraudulent and every story he tells is a lie. He works diligently to trick his fellow devils in Hell by having Beelzebub present Satan's own plan of action.

Satan's character—or our perception of his character—changes significantly from Book I to his final appearance in Book X. In Book I he is a strong, imposing figure with great abilities as a leader and public statesmen, whereas by the poem's end he slinks back to Hell in serpent form. Satan's gradual degradation is dramatized by the sequence of different shapes he assumes. He begins the poem as a just-fallen angel of enormous stature, looks like a comet or meteor as he leaves Hell, then disguises himself as a more humble cherub, then as a cormorant, a toad, and finally a snake. His ability to reason and argue also deteriorates. In Book I, he persuades the devils to agree to his plan. In Book IV, however, he reasons to himself that the Hell he feels inside of him is reason to do more evil. When he returns to Earth again, he believes that Earth is more beautiful than Heaven, and that he may be able to live on Earth after all. Satan, removed from Heaven long enough to forget its unparalleled grandeur, is completely demented, coming to believe in his own lies. He is a picture of incessant intellectual activity without the ability to think morally. Once a powerful angel, he has become blinded to God's grace, forever unable to reconcile his past with his eternal punishment.

ADAM

Adam is a strong, intelligent, and rational character possessed of a remarkable relationship with God. In fact, before the fall, he is as perfect as a human being can be. He has an enormous capacity for reason, and can understand the most sophisticated ideas instantly. He can converse with Raphael as a near-equal, and understand Raphael's stories readily. But after the fall, his conversation with Michael during his visions is significantly one-sided. Also, his self-doubt and anger after the fall demonstrate his new ability to indulge in rash and irrational attitudes. As a result of the fall, he loses his pure reason and intellect.

Adam's greatest weakness is his love for Eve. He falls in love with her immediately upon seeing her, and confides to Raphael that his attraction to her is almost overwhelming. Though Raphael warns him to keep his affections in check, Adam is powerless to prevent his love from overwhelming his reason. After Eve eats from the Tree of Knowledge, he quickly does the same, realizing that if she is doomed, he must follow her into doom as well if he wants to avoid losing her. Eve has become his companion for life, and he is unwilling to part with her even if that means disobeying God.

Adam's curiosity and hunger for knowledge is another weakness. The questions he asks of Raphael about creation and the universe may suggest a growing temptation to eat from the Tree of Knowledge. But like his physical attraction to Eve, Adam is able to partly avoid this temptation. It is only through Eve that his temptations become unavoidable.

EVE

Created to be Adam's mate, Eve is inferior to Adam, but only slightly. She surpasses Adam only in her beauty. She falls in love with her own image when she sees her reflection in a body of water. Ironically, her greatest asset produces her most serious weakness, vanity. After Satan compliments her on her beauty and godliness, he easily persuades her to eat from the Tree of Knowledge.

Aside from her beauty, Eve's intelligence and spiritual purity is constantly tested. She is not unintelligent, but she is not ambitious to learn, content to be guided by Adam as God intended. As a result, she does not become more intelligent or learned as the story progresses, though she does attain the beginning of wisdom by the end of the poem. Her lack of learning is partly due to her absence for most of Raphael's discussions with Adam in Books V, VI, and VII, and she also does not see the visions Michael shows Adam in Books XI and XII. Her absence from these important exchanges shows that she feels it is not her place to seek knowledge independently; she wants to hear Raphael's stories through Adam later. The one instance in which she deviates from her passive role, telling Adam to trust her on her own and then seizing the fruit of the Tree of Knowledge, is disastrous.

Eve's strengths are her capacity for love, emotion, and forebearance. She persuades Adam to stay with her after the fall, and Adam in turn dissuades her from committing suicide, as they begin to work together as a powerful unit. Eve complements Adam's strengths and corrects his weaknesses. Thus, Milton does not denigrate all women through his depiction of Eve. Rather he explores the role of women in his society and the positive and important role he felt they could offer in the divine union of marriage.

GOD

An omniscient, omnipresent, and omnipotent character who knows everything before it happens. Attempting to present such an unimaginable character accurately, Milton appropriates several of God's biblical speeches into his speeches in *Paradise Lost*. God loves his creation and strongly defends humankind's free will. He presents his love through his Son, who performs his will justly and mercifully.

God, in *Paradise Lost,* is less a developed character than a personification of abstract ideas. He is unknowable to humankind and to some extent lacks emotion and depth. He has no weaknesses, embodies pure reason, and is always just. He explains why certain events happen, like Satan's decision to corrupt Adam and Eve, tells his angels what will happen next, and gives his reasoning behind his actions in theological terms. God allows evil to occur, but he will make good out of evil. His plan to save humankind by offering his Son shows his unwavering control over Satan.

THE SON

For Milton, the Son is the manifestation of God in action. While God the Father stays in the realm of Heaven, the Son performs the difficult tasks of banishing Satan and his rebel angels, creating the universe and humankind, and punishing Satan, Adam and Eve with justice and mercy. The Son physically connects God the Father with his creation. Together they form a complete and perfect God.

The Son personifies love and compassion. After the fall, he pities Adam and Eve and gives them clothing to help diminish their shame. His decision to volunteer to die for humankind shows his dedication and selflessness. The final vision that Adam sees in Book XII is of the Son's (or Jesus') sacrifice on the cross—through this vision, the Son is able to calm Adam's worries for humankind and give Adam and Eve restored hope as they venture out of Paradise.

CHARACTER ANALYSIS

Themes, Motifs & Symbols

Themes

Themes are the fundamental and often universal ideas explored in a literary work.

The Importance of Obedience to God

The first words of *Paradise Lost* state that the poem's main theme will be "Man's first Disobedience." Milton narrates the story of Adam and Eve's disobedience, explains how and why it happens, and places the story within the larger context of Satan's rebellion and Jesus' resurrection. Raphael tells Adam about Satan's disobedience in an effort to give him a firm grasp of the threat that Satan and humankind's disobedience poses. In essence, *Paradise Lost* presents two moral paths that one can take after disobedience: the downward spiral of increasing sin and degradation, represented by Satan, and the road to redemption, represented by Adam and Eve.

While Adam and Eve are the first humans to disobey God, Satan is the first of all God's creation to disobey. His decision to rebel comes only from himself—he was not persuaded or provoked by others. Also, his decision to continue to disobey God after his fall into Hell ensures that God will not forgive him. Adam and Eve, on the other hand, decide to repent for their sins and seek forgiveness. Unlike Satan, Adam and Eve understand that their disobedience to God does not know that their disobedience will be corrected through generations of toil on Earth. This path is obviously the correct one to take: the visions in Books XI and XII demonstrate that obedience to God, even after repeated falls, can lead to humankind's salvation.

The Hierarchical Nature of the Universe

Paradise Lost is about hierarchy as much as it is about obedience. The layout of the universe—with Heaven above, Hell below, and Earth in the middle—presents the universe as a hierarchy based on proximity to God and his grace. This spatial hierarchy leads to a social hierarchy of angels, humans, animals, and devils: the Son is closest to God, with the archangels and cherubs behind him. Adam and Eve and Earth's animals come next, with Satan and the other fallen angels following last. To obey God is to respect this hierarchy.

Satan refuses to honor the Son as his superior, thereby questioning God's hierarchy. As the angels in Satan's camp rebel, they hope to beat God and thereby dissolve what they believe to be an unfair hierarchy in Heaven. When the Son and the good angels defeat the rebel angels, the rebels are punished by being banished far away from Heaven. At least, Satan argues later, they can make their own hierarchy in Hell, but they are nevertheless subject to God's overall hierarchy, in which they are ranked the lowest. Satan continues to disobey God and his hierarchy as he seeks to corrupt mankind.

Likewise, humankind's disobedience is a corruption of God's hierarchy. Before the fall, Adam and Eve treat the visiting angels with proper respect and acknowledgement of their closeness to God, and Eve embraces the subservient role allotted to her in her marriage. God and Raphael both instruct Adam that Eve is slightly farther removed from God's grace than Adam because she was created to serve both God and him. When Eve persuades Adam to let her work alone, she challenges him, her superior, and he yields to her, his inferior. Again, as Adam eats from the fruit, he knowingly defies God by obeying Eve and his inner instinct instead of God and his reason. Adam's visions in Books XI and XII show more examples of this disobedience to God and the universe's hierarchy, but also demonstrate that with the Son's sacrifice, this hierarchy will be restored once again.

THE FALL AS PARTLY FORTUNATE

After he sees the vision of Christ's redemption of humankind in Book XII, Adam refers to his own sin as a *felix culpa* or "happy fault," suggesting that the fall of humankind, while originally seeming an unmitigated catastrophe, does in fact bring good with it. Adam and Eve's disobedience allows God to show his mercy and temperance in their punishments and his eternal providence toward humankind. This display of love and compassion, given through the Son, is a gift to humankind. Humankind must now experience pain and death, but humans can also experience mercy, salvation, and grace in ways they would not have been able to had they not disobeyed. While humankind has fallen from grace, individuals can redeem and save themselves through continued devotion and obedience to God. The salvation of humankind, in the form of The Son's

THEMES

sacrifice and resurrection, can begin to restore humankind to its former state. In other words, good will come of sin and death, and humankind will eventually be rewarded. This fortunate result justifies God's reasoning and explains his ultimate plan for humankind.

MOTIFS

Motifs are recurring structures, contrasts, or literary devices that can help to develop and inform the text's major themes.

LIGHT AND DARK

Opposites abound in *Paradise Lost,* including Heaven and Hell, God and Satan, and good and evil. Milton's uses imagery of light and darkness to express all of these opposites. Angels are physically described in terms of light, whereas devils are generally described by their shadowy darkness. Milton also uses light to symbolize God and God's grace. In his invocation in Book III, Milton asks that he be filled with this light so he can tell his divine story accurately and persuasively. While the absence of light in Hell and in Satan himself represents the absence of God and his grace.

THE GEOGRAPHY OF THE UNIVERSE

Milton divides the universe into four major regions: glorious Heaven, dreadful Hell, confusing Chaos, and a young and vulnerable Earth in between. The opening scenes that take place in Hell give the reader immediate context as to Satan's plot against God and humankind. The intermediate scenes in Heaven, in which God tells the angels of his plans, provide a philosophical and theological context for the story. Then, with these established settings of good and evil, light and dark, much of the action occurs in between on Earth. The powers of good and evil work against each other on this new battlefield of Earth. Satan fights God by tempting Adam and Eve, while God shows his love and mercy through the Son's punishment of Adam and Eve.

Milton believes that any other information concerning the geography of the universe is unimportant. Milton acknowledges both the possibility that the sun revolves around the Earth and that the Earth revolves around the sun, without coming down on one side or the other. Raphael asserts that it does not matter which revolves around which, demonstrating that Milton's cosmology is based on the religious message he wants to convey, rather than on the findings of contemporaneous science or astronomy.

CONVERSATION AND CONTEMPLATION

One common objection raised by readers of *Paradise Lost* is that the poem contains relatively little action. Milton sought to divert the reader's attention from heroic battles and place it on the conversations and contemplations of his characters. Conversations comprise almost five complete books of *Paradise Lost,* close to half of the text. Milton's narrative emphasis on conversation conveys the importance he attached to conversation and contemplation, two pursuits that he believed were of fundamental importance for a moral person. As with Adam and Raphael, and again with Adam and Michael, the sharing of ideas allows two people to share and spread God's message. Likewise, pondering God and his grace allows a person to become closer to God and more obedient. Adam constantly contemplates God before the fall, whereas Satan contemplates only himself. After the fall, Adam and Eve must learn to maintain their conversation and contemplation if they hope to make their own happiness outside of Paradise.

SYMBOLS

Symbols are objects, characters, figures, or colors used to represent abstract ideas or concepts.

THE SCALES IN THE SKY

As Satan prepares to fight Gabriel when he is discovered in Paradise, God causes the image of a pair of golden scales to appear in the sky. On one side of the scales, he puts the consequences of Satan's running away, and on the other he puts the consequences of Satan's staying and fighting with Gabriel. The side that shows him staying and fighting flies up, signifying its lightness and worthlessness. These scales symbolize the fact that God and Satan are not truly on opposite sides of a struggle—God is all-powerful, and Satan and Gabriel *both* derive all of their power from Him. God's scales force Satan to realize the futility of taking arms against one of God's angels again.

ADAM'S WREATH

The wreath that Adam makes as he and Eve work separately in Book IX is symbolic in several ways. First, it represents his love for her and his attraction to her. But as he is about to give the wreath to her, his shock in noticing that she has eaten from the Tree of Knowledge makes him drop it to the ground. His dropping of the wreath symbolizes that his love and attraction to Eve is falling away. His image of her as a spiritual companion has been shattered completely, as he realizes her fallen state. The fallen wreath represents the loss of pure love.

SYMBOLS

Summary & Analysis

Book I, lines 1–26

Summary: Lines 1–26: The Prologue and Invocation

Milton opens *Paradise Lost* by formally declaring his poem's subject: humankind's first act of disobedience toward God, and the consequences that followed from it. The act is Adam and Eve's eating of the forbidden fruit of the Tree of Knowledge, as told in Genesis, the first book of the Bible. In the first line, Milton refers to the outcome of Adam and Eve's sin as the "fruit" of the forbidden tree, punning on the actual apple and the figurative fruits of their actions. Milton asserts that this original sin brought death to human beings for the first time, causing us to lose our home in paradise until Jesus comes to restore humankind to its former position of purity.

Milton's speaker invokes the muse, a mystical source of poetic inspiration, to sing about these subjects through him, but he makes it clear that he refers to a different muse from the muses who traditionally inspired classical poets by specifying that his muse inspired Moses to receive the Ten Commandments and write Genesis. Milton's muse is the Holy Spirit, which inspired the Christian Bible, not one of the nine classical muses who reside on Mount Helicon—the "Aonian mount" of I.15. He says that his poem, like his muse, will fly above those of the Classical poets and accomplish things never attempted before, because his source of inspiration is greater than theirs. Then he invokes the Holy Spirit, asking it to fill him with knowledge of the beginning of the world, because the Holy Spirit was the active force in creating the universe.

Milton's speaker announces that he wants to be inspired with this sacred knowledge because he wants to show his fellow man that the fall of humankind into sin and death was part of God's greater plan, and that God's plan is justified.

Analysis

The beginning of *Paradise Lost* is similar in gravity and seriousness to the book from which Milton takes much of his story: the Book of Genesis, the first book of the Bible. The Bible begins with the story of the world's creation, and Milton's epic begins in a similar vein, alluding to the creation of the world by the Holy Spirit. The first two sentences, or twenty-six lines, of *Paradise Lost* are extremely compressed, containing a great deal of information about Milton's reasons for writing his epic, his subject matter, and his attitudes toward his subject. In these two sentences, Milton invokes his muse, which is actually the Holy Spirit rather than one of the nine muses. By invoking a muse, but differentiating it from traditional muses, Milton manages to tell us quite a lot about how he sees his project. In the first place, an invocation of the muse at the beginning of an epic is conventional, so Milton is acknowledging his awareness of Homer, Virgil, and later poets, and signaling that he has mastered their format and wants to be part of their tradition. But by identifying his muse as the divine spirit that inspired the Bible and created the world, he shows that his ambitions go far beyond joining the club of Homer and Virgil. Milton's epic will surpass theirs, drawing on a more fundamental source of truth and dealing with matters of more fundamental importance to human beings. At the same time, however, Milton's invocation is extremely humble, expressing his utter dependence on God's grace in speaking through him. Milton thus begins his poem with a mixture of towering ambition and humble self-effacement, simultaneously tipping his hat to his poetic forebears and promising to soar above them for God's glorification.

Milton's approach to the invocation of the muse, in which he takes a classical literary convention and reinvents it from a Christian perspective, sets the pattern for all of *Paradise Lost*. For example, when he catalogs the prominent devils in Hell and explains the various names they are known by and which cults worshipped them, he makes devils of many gods whom the Greeks, Ammonites, and other ancient peoples worshipped. In other words, the great gods of the classical world have become—according to Milton—fallen angels. His poem purports to tell of these gods' original natures, before they infected humankind in the form of false gods. Through such comparisons with the classical epic poems, Milton is quick to demonstrate that the scope of his epic poem is much greater than those of the classical poets, and that his worldview and inspiration is more fundamentally true and all-encompassing than theirs. The setting, or world, of Milton's epic is large enough to include those smaller, classical worlds. Milton also displays his world's superiority while reducing those classical epics to the level of old, nearly forgotten stories. For example, the nine muses of classical epics still exist on Mount Helicon in the world of *Paradise Lost,* but

Milton's muse haunts other areas and has the ability to fly above those other, less-powerful classical Muses. Thus Milton both makes himself the authority on antiquity and subordinates it to his Christian worldview.

The *Iliad* and the *Aeneid* are the great epic poems of Greek and Latin, respectively, and Milton emulates them because he intends *Paradise Lost* to be the first English epic. Milton wants to make glorious art out of the English language the way the other epics had done for their languages. Not only must a great epic be long and poetically well-constructed, its subject must be significant and original, its form strict and serious, and its aims noble and heroic. In Milton's view, the story he will tell is the most original story known to man, as it is the first story of the world and of the first human beings. Also, while Homer and Virgil only chronicled the journey of heroic men, like Achilles or Aeneas, Milton chronicles the tragic journey of *all* men—the result of humankind's disobedience. Milton goes so far as to say that he hopes to "justify," or explain, God's mysterious plan for humankind. Homer and Virgil describe great wars between men, but Milton tells the story of the most epic battle possible: the battle between God and Satan, good and evil.

BOOK I, LINES 27–722

SUMMARY: LINES 27–722: SATAN AND HELL

Immediately after the prologue, Milton raises the question of how Adam and Eve's disobedience occurred and explains that their actions were partly due to a serpent's deception. This serpent is Satan, and the poem joins him and his followers in Hell, where they have just been cast after being defeated by God in Heaven.

Satan lies stunned beside his second-in-command, Beelzebub, in a lake of fire that gives off darkness instead of light. Breaking the awful silence, Satan bemoans their terrible position, but does not repent of his rebellion against God, suggesting that they might gather their forces for another attack. Beelzebub is doubtful; he now believes that God cannot be overpowered. Satan does not fully contradict this assessment, but suggests that they could at least pervert God's good works to evil purposes. The two devils then rise up and, spreading their wings, fly over to the dry land next to the flaming lake. But they can undertake this action only because God has allowed them to loose their chains. All of the devils were formerly angels who chose to follow Satan in his rebellion, and God still intends to turn their evil deeds toward the good.

Once out of the lake, Satan becomes more optimistic about their situation. He calls the rest of the fallen angels, his legions, to join him on land. They immediately obey and, despite their wounds and suffering, fly up to gather on the plain. Milton lists some of the more notable of the angels whose names have been erased from the books of Heaven, noting that later, in the time of man, many of these devils come to be worshipped as gods.

Among these are Moloch, who is later known as a god requiring human sacrifices, and Belial, a lewd and lustful god. Still in war gear, these fallen angels have thousands of banners raised and their shields and spears in hand. Even in defeat, they are an awesome army to behold.

Satan's unrepentant evil nature is unwavering. Even cast down in defeat, he does not consider changing his ways: he insists to his fellow devils that their delight will be in doing evil, not good. In particular, as he explains to Beelzebub, he wishes to pervert God's will and find a way to make evil out of good. It is not easy for Satan to maintain this determination; the battle has just demonstrated God's overwhelming power, and the devils could not even have lifted themselves off the lake of fire unless God had allowed it. God allows it precisely because he intends to turn their evil designs toward a greater good in the end. Satan's envy of the Son's chosen status led him to rebel and consequently to be condemned. His continued envy and search for freedom leads him to believe that he would rather be a king in Hell than a servant in Heaven. Satan's pride has caused him to believe that his own free intellect is as great as God's will. Satan remarks that the mind can make its own Hell out of Heaven, or in his case, its own Heaven out of Hell.

Satan addresses his comrades and acknowledges their shame in falling to the heavenly forces, but urges them to gather in order to consider whether another war is feasible. Instantly, the legions of devils dig into the bowels of the ground, unearthing gold and other minerals. With their inhuman powers they construct a great temple in a short time. It is called Pandemonium (which means "all the demons" in Latin), and the hundreds of thousands of demonic troops gather there to hold a summit. Being spirits, they can easily shrink from huge winged creatures to the smallest size. Compacting themselves, they enter Pandemonium, and the debate begins.

ANALYSIS

Throughout the first two or three books of *Paradise Lost,* Satan seems as if he's the hero of the poem. This is partly because the focus of the poem is all on him, but it is also because the first books establish his struggle—he finds himself defeated and banished from Heaven, and sets about establishing a new course for himself and those he leads. Typically, the hero or protagonist of *any* narrative, epic poem or otherwise, is a person who struggles to accomplish something. Milton plays against our expectations by spending the first quarter of his epic telling us about the antagonist rather than the protagonist, so that when we meet Adam and Eve, we will have a more profound sense of what they are up against. But even when the focus of the poem shifts to Adam and Eve, Satan remains the most active force in the story.

One important way in which the narrator develops our picture of Satan—and gives us the impression that he is a hero—is through *epic similes,* lengthy and developed comparisons that tell us how big and powerful Satan is. For example, when Satan is lying on the burning lake, Milton compares him to the titans who waged war upon Jove in Greek mythology. Then, at greater length, he compares him to a Leviathan, or whale, that is so huge that sailors mistake it for an island and fix their anchor to it. In other epics, these sorts of similes are used to establish the great size or strength of characters, and on the surface these similes seem to do the same thing. At the same time, however, the effect of these similes is to unsettle us, making us aware that we really do not know how big Satan is at all. No one knows how big the titans were, because they were defeated before the age of man. The image of the Leviathan does not give us a well-defined sense of his size, because the whole point of the image is that the Leviathan's size generates deception and confusion.

More than anything, the similes used to describe Satan make us aware of the fact that size is relative, and that we don't know how big anything in Hell is—the burning lake, the hill, Pandemonium, etc. Milton drives this fact home at the end of Book I with a tautology: while most of the devils shrink in size to enter Pandemonium, the important ones sit "far within / And in their own dimensions like themselves" (I.792–793). In other words, they were however big they were, but we have no way of knowing how big that was. Finally, it is important to note that the first description of Satan's size is the biggest we will ever see him. From that point on, Satan assumes many shapes and is compared to numerous creatures, but his size and stature steadily diminishes. The uncertainty created by these similes creates a sense of irony—perhaps Satan isn't so great after all.

The devils in *Paradise Lost* are introduced to the story here in Book I in almost a parody of how Homer introduces great warriors in the *Iliad*. The irony of these descriptions lies in the fact that while these devils seem heroic and noteworthy in certain ways, they just lost the war in Heaven. As frightening and vividly presented as these creatures are, they did not succeed in killing a single angel.

In Book I, Milton presents Satan primarily as a military hero, and the council of devils as a council of war. In doing so, he makes *Paradise Lost* resonate with earlier epics, which all center around military heroes and their exploits. At the same time, Milton presents an implicit critique of a literary culture that glorifies war and warriors. Satan displays all of the virtues of a great warrior such as Achilles or Odysseus. He is courageous, undaunted, refusing to yield in the face of impossible odds, and able to stir his followers to follow him in brave and violent exploits. Milton is clearly aware of what he's doing in making Satan somewhat appealing in the early chapters. By drawing us into sympathizing with and admiring Satan, Milton forces us to question why we admire martial prowess and pride in literary characters. Ultimately he attempts to show that the Christian virtues of obedience, humility, and forbearance are more important.

BOOK II

SUMMARY

Satan opens the debate in Pandemonium by claiming that Heaven is not yet lost, and that the fallen angels (or devils) might rise up stronger in another battle if they work together. He opens the floor, and the pro-war devil Moloch speaks first. Moloch was one of the fiercest fighters in the war in Heaven, and he anxiously pleads for another open war, this time armed with the weapons of Hell. He reasons that nothing, even their destruction, could be worse than Hell, and so they have nothing to lose by another attack. Belial speaks up to contradict him. He eloquently offers calm reason to counter Moloch's fiery temper, and claims that God has not yet punished them as fiercely as he might if they went to war with him again. After all, they are no longer chained to the fiery lake, which was their previous and worse punishment; since God may one day forgive them, it is better that they live with what they now have. But peace is not really what he advocates; rather, Belial uses his considerable intelligence to find excuses to prevent further war and to advocate lassitude and inaction. Mammon speaks up next, and refuses to ever bow down to God again. He prefers to peacefully advance their freedom and asks the devils to be industrious in Hell. Through hard work, the devils can make Hell their own kingdom to mimic Heaven. This argument meets with the greatest support among the legions of the fallen, who receive his suggestion with applause.

Quiet falls upon the crowd as the respected Beelzebub begins to speak. He also prefers freedom to servitude under God, but counsels a different course of action than those previously advocated. Apparently, he says, rumors have been circulating in Heaven about a new world that is to be created, to be filled with a race called Man, whom God will favor more than the angels. Beelzebub advises, at Satan's secret behest, that they seek their revenge by destroying or corrupting this new beloved race. The rest of the devils agree and vote unanimously in favor of this plan. They must now send a scout to find out about this new world, and in a feat of staged heroics, Satan volunteers himself.

While the other devils break into groups to discuss the outcome of the debate and to build other structures, Satan flies off to find Hell's gate. When he approaches, he sees that it is actually nine gates—three each of brass, iron, and adamantine—and that two strange shapes stand guard in front. One looks like a woman down to her waist, but below has the form of a serpent, with a pack of howling dogs around her waist. The other is only a dark shape. Satan chooses to confront the shape, demanding passage through the gates. They are about to do battle when the woman-beast cries out. She explains to Satan who she and her companion are and how they came to be, claiming that they are in fact Satan's own offspring. While Satan was still an angel, she sprang forth from his head, and was named Sin. Satan then incestuously impregnated her, and she gave birth to a ghostly son named Death. Death in turn raped his mother Sin, begetting the dogs that now torment her. Sin and Death were then assigned to guard the gate of Hell and hold its keys.

Apparently, Satan had forgotten these events. Now he speaks less violently to them and explains his plot against God. After Satan's persuasion, they are more than eager to help him. Sin unlocks the great gates, which open into the vast dark abyss of night. Satan flies out but then begins to fall, until a cloud of fire catches and carries him. He hears a great tumult of noise and makes his way toward it;

it is Chaos, ruler of the abyss. Chaos is joined by his consort Night, with Confusion, Discord and others at their side. Satan explains his plan to Chaos as well. He asks for help, saying that in return he will reclaim the territory of the new world, thus returning more of the universe to disorder. Chaos agrees and points out the way to where the Earth has recently been created. With great difficulty, Satan moves onward, and Sin and Death follow far behind, building a bridge from Hell to Earth on which evil spirits can travel to tempt mortals.

ANALYSIS

Just as Book I may be seen as a parody of military heroism, the devils' debate in Book II can be read as a parody of political debate. Their nonviolent and democratic decision to wreak the destruction of humankind shows the corruption of fallen reason, which can make evil appear as good. Milton depicts the devils' organization ironically, as if he were commending it. Satan, for example, diplomatically urges others "to union, and firm faith, and firm accord," making Hell's newly formed government sound legitimate and powerful when it is in fact grossly illegitimate and powerless (II.36). It is possible that Milton here satirizes politicians and political debates in general, not just corrupt politicians. Certainly, Milton had witnessed enough violent political struggles in his time to give him cause to demonize politicians as a species. Clearly, the debate in Hell weighs only different evils, rather than bringing its participants closer to truth.

This scene also demonstrates Milton's cynicism about political institutions and organizations. The devils' behavior suggests that political power tends to corrupt individuals who possess it. Even learned politicians, as Belial is here in Book II, who possess great powers of reason and intellectual discourse, have the power to deceive the less-educated public. In his other writings, Milton argues that political and religious organizations have the potential to do evil things in the name of order and union. After the debate in Hell is concluded, the object of parody shifts to philosophers and religious thinkers. Following the debate, the devils break into groups, some of which continue to speak and argue without any resolution or amenable conclusion. Similar debates over the sources of evil and of political authority were fiercely contested in Milton's time. Milton calls the devils' discussions "vain wisdom all, and false philosophy," a criticism which he extends in his other writings to the words of the religious leaders of his time (II.565).

After Beelzebub takes the floor, it becomes clear that the caucus has been a foregone conclusion. Satan lets the sides rhetorically engage each other before he announces through Beelzebub the plan he had all along. Satan and Beelzebub conspire to win the argument, and do, without any of the other devils recognizing the fraud. Satan's volunteering to be the scout then silences all possible dissent, since he is heralded as the leader of Hell. Here again is a parody of Hell mimicking Heaven: Satan offers to sacrifice himself for the good of the other devils, in a twisted imitation of Christ. The parallel is made even more blatant when Sin cries out to Satan at the gate of Hell: "O father, what intends thy hand . . . against thy only son?" (II.727–728). Sin's statement foreshadows how God will send his only Son to die, for the good of the humankind. Satan believes he is free, and both Belial and Mammon celebrate the freedom of the devils even in Hell, and yet we see that they have no power to do anything except distort Heavenly things, twisting them into evil, empty imitations.

Satan's encounter with Sin and Death is an allegory, in which the three characters and their relationships represent abstract ideas. Sin is the first child of Satan, brought to life by Satan's disobedience. Since Satan is the first of God's creations to disobey, he personifies disobedience, and the fact that Sin is his daughter suggests that all sins arise from disobedience and ingratitude toward God. To those who behold her birth, she is first frightening but then seems strangely attractive, suggesting the seductive allure of sin to the ordinary individual. Sin dwells alone and in utter torment, representing the ultimate fate of the sinner. That Death is Sin's offspring indicates Milton's belief that death is not simply a biological fact of life but rather a punishment for sin and disobedience, a punishment that nobody escapes.

Book III

Summary
Book III opens with a second invocation to his muse, this time addressed to "holy light" (III.1). Milton asks that the heavenly light shine inside him and illuminate his mind with divine knowledge so that he can share this knowledge with his readers.

The scene shifts to Heaven, where God has been watching all of the events in Hell with his Son sitting at his right hand. He sees Satan flying up toward the new Earth and the parents of mankind. At the same time, he sees everything that will happen because of it, perceiving past, present, and future simultaneously. He sees that man will fall, of his own fault, because God gave him free will—yet without that will, man would not be capable of sincere love. Man would merely go through the motions. While it would be just to punish man for his own actions, God determines that he will act primarily out of love and mercy. The Son, full of compassion, praises God for his kindness toward man, but asks how mercy can be given without destroying justice. God answers that a suitable sacrifice must be made: someone worthy must offer to die to pay for man's sin. The angelic choirs are silent, but the Son immediately offers himself. He will become mortal so that God can yield to Death and conquer Hell. God is overjoyed, even though he will be giving up his son, because he knows that it is good to sacrifice his son for the salvation of the human race, in order for justice and mercy to be served. Those that have faith in the Son will be redeemed, but those who do not accept grace will still be doomed to Hell. The choirs of angels now break into a song of praise extolling the goodness of both Father and Son, which will turn a sorrowful deed into greater glory for both God and man.

The story returns to Satan, who lands on Earth in what is now China. There are not yet any living things there, or any of the works of man that will eventually distract man's mind from God. At length, Satan sees a high-reaching structure in the distance, an enormous kingly gate in the sky with stairs leading all the way down to Earth. This gate guards Heaven, which was at that time visible from Earth. Flying over to it, Satan climbs up a few steps to get a better view. He sees the new creation in all its glory, but can only feel jealousy. He does not stay put for long, though: he is drawn by the golden sun, hanging above the green and lush land, and flies toward it. There he sees an angel standing on a hill. To deceive him, Satan changes to a cherub, or low-ranking angel. Recognizing the other angel as the Archangel Uriel, Satan approaches and addresses him. Satan claims to have just come down from Heaven, full of curiosity about the new world he has been hearing so much about, and curious about its inhabitants. Satan's transformation and his speech are so flawless that even Uriel cannot see through the subterfuge. The Archangel is pleased that a young angel is showing so much zeal to find out about the world that God brought out of the Chaos from earth, air, wind and fire. He happily points out the way to Paradise, where Adam lives. After giving his due respects, Satan flies off with dark intentions.

ANALYSIS

As the narrative of *Paradise Lost* shifts from its sustained focus on Hell and Satan and begins to present glimpses of Heaven and God, we may feel that the story loses some of the intense interest and appeal that it began with. The discussion in Heaven is moving and theologically interesting, but the parts of the poem treating the evil designs of Satan are written with more potency and rhetorical vigor. The characters in Heaven play a relatively passive role, watching the story unfold, while Satan actively and endlessly devises his evil machinations. Moreover, the sinful, evil characters hold our attention more easily than the pure and virtuous ones. Satan appears to be the active hero, struggling for his personal desires, and God may seem rather dull. These observations, however, are beside the point that Milton hopes to prove to his readers: God's reason and grace rule the universe and control all of those who live there.

The encounter between Satan and Uriel demonstrates Satan's capacity for deception and fraud, as he subverts Uriel's role as a guardian by disguising himself as a cherub. Uriel is unable to recognize Satan in part because he does not believe it possible that Satan would be lurking around. As a devout and virtuous angel, Uriel is unable to recognize evil even when it presents itself right in front of him. Through Satan's deception of Uriel, Milton shows the significance of the sin of fraud, or hypocrisy. Fraud is an especially damaging sin because it is invisible to others, hurting them in ways they are not even aware of. In the *Inferno*, Dante maintains that fraud is the worst of all man's sins. Milton goes almost as far in showing that leading innocent people to evil is much worse than leading yourself to evil.

Milton reveals his own personal theological positions in Book III. Through God's initial speech, for example, Milton discards the orthodox Calvinist position of predestination. Omniscient God, seeing the fall in the future, says that men cannot blame God for their fate, or for acts of evil or bad luck, insisting that man possesses free will, even though God can foresee what they will do. God's speech here contradicts the Calvinist belief, held by most of Milton's fellow Puritans, that the fate of every man's soul is decided before birth. Milton refuses to abandon his belief in free will, insisting that man must have free will in order to prove his sincere love for God. This balance between free will and virtue is a paradox—man is free to choose, but only truly free when he chooses the good.

Milton had to confront certain problems inherent in any attempt to represent beings and events outside of time and human understanding. To have God and the Son appear as separate characters in a work of fiction poses particular problems and risks in terms of logical consistency. There may not be a completely coherent way to represent God and the Son as characters who are both independent and human-like, but at the same time consubstantial, omniscient, omnipresent, and omnipotent. It was extremely ambitious of Milton to risk heresy by putting words in God's mouth, and he lessens this risk by incorporating numerous biblical allusions into the speeches of God and the Son.

By making God and the Son two different characters, Milton asserts that they are essentially separate but equal entities. Milton did not believe in the Holy Trinity completely, and believed that the Son was created after God, not coeternally. The relationship between God and the Son is not fully revealed. Appearing as separate characters with separate comments, they may still share a mind. Some actions, like God's plea for a volunteer, and the Son's subsequent volunteering, argue that they do not share a single mind. God asks for a volunteer, yet he must know ahead of time that his Son will be the only volunteer. The precise nature of the relationship between the two remains mysterious.

BOOK IV

SUMMARY

Satan lands atop Mount Niphates, just north of Paradise, the Garden of Eden. He becomes gripped with doubt about the task in front of him; seeing the beauty and innocence of Earth has reminded him of what he once was. He even briefly considers whether he could be forgiven if he repented. But Hell follows him wherever he goes—Satan is actually the embodiment of Hell. If he asks the Father for forgiveness, he knows it would be a false confession; he reasons that if he returned to Heaven, he still could not bear to bow down. Knowing redemption or salvation cannot be granted to him, he resolves to continue to commit acts of sin and evil. He does not notice that during his internal debate, he has inadvertently revealed his devilish nature. He is observed by Uriel, the archangel he tricked into pointing the way. Uriel notices his conflicting facial expressions, and since all cherubs have permanent looks of joy on their faces, Uriel concludes that Satan cannot be a cherub.

Satan now approaches Eden, which is surrounded by a great thicket wall. He easily leaps over it like a wolf entering a sheep's pen.

Inside he sees an idyllic world, with all varieties of animals and trees. He can see the tallest of the trees, the Tree of Life—and next to it, the forbidden Tree of Knowledge. He perches himself on the Tree of Life, disguised as a cormorant, a large sea bird. Finally, he notices two creatures walking erect among the other animals. They walk naked without shame, and work pleasantly, tending the garden. Satan's pain and envy intensifies as he sees this new beautiful race, created after he and his legions fell. He could have loved them, but now, his damnation will be revenged through their destruction. He continues to watch them, and the man, Adam, speaks. He tells Eve not to complain of the work they have to do but to be obedient to God, since God has given them so many blessings, and only one constraint: they must not eat the fruit of the Tree of Knowledge. Eve agrees wholeheartedly, and they embrace.

Eve tells Adam of her first awakening as she came to life and how she wondered who and where she was. She found a river and followed it upstream to its source. Her path led to a clear, smooth lake, and Eve looked into the lake, seeing an image in its surface, which she soon discovers is her own. She hears a voice explaining to her that she was made out of Adam, and with him she will become of mother of the human race. Overlooking Adam and Eve, Satan sees his opportunity. If the Father has given them a rule to follow, then they might be persuaded to break it. He leaves the two for a while, going off to learn more from other angels.

Meanwhile, Uriel comes before the Archangel Gabriel, at the gate of Eden, and tells him about the shape-changing spirit that he saw from the hilltop. They both suspect that it might be one of the fallen ones. Gabriel promises that if the spirit is in the garden, they will find it by morning. Around this time, Adam and Eve finish their day's work. They go to their leafy bower, praising God and each other for their blissful life, and after a short prayer, they lie together—making love without sin, because lust had not yet tainted their natures.

Night falls, and Gabriel sends search parties into the Garden. Two of his angels find Satan, disguised as a toad, whispering into the ear of Eve as she sleeps. They pull him before Gabriel, who recognizes him, and demands to know what he is doing in Paradise. Satan at first feigns innocence, as they have no proof that he means harm. But Gabriel knows him to be a liar, and threatens to drag him back to Hell. Enraged by this threat, Satan prepares to fight him. The two square off for a decisive battle, but a sign from Heaven—the appearance in the sky of a pair of golden scales—stops them. Satan recognizes the sign as meaning he could not win, and flies off.

ANALYSIS

As Book IV opens, Milton presents Satan as a character deeply affected by envy and despair. Earlier in the poem, Satan seems perfectly confident in his rebellion and evil plans. His feeling of despair at the beauty of Paradise temporarily impairs this confidence. While in Hell, Satan tells himself that his mind could make its own Heaven out of Hell, but now he realizes that the reverse is true. As close to Heaven as he is, he cannot help but feel out of place, because he brings Hell with him wherever he goes. For Satan, Hell is not simply a place, but rather a state of mind brought on by a lack of connection with God. Satan's despondent recognition of this fact corresponds with what Milton sees as the worst sin of all: despair. If even this beautiful new world cannot make Satan forget Hell, then he can never hope to seek forgiveness and return to Heaven. As the Bible says, the one sin that cannot be forgiven is despairing of forgiveness; if one cannot even ask for mercy, it cannot be granted. Satan realizes this, and decides that the only course of action is to enjoy his own wickedness, and pursue it with all his strength. Milton preempts the crucial question of whether Satan could have successfully repented back in Book III. There, God said that he would give grace to humankind because Satan would prompt humankind's sin. But he would not help the fallen angels, and especially Satan, because their sin came out of themselves and from no other source.

Satan's continuing process of degradation is reflected in his use of progressively despicable, lowly disguises. Through these first three books of *Paradise Lost,* Satan's physical presence takes many different forms. In Book I, he is a monumental figure so large that the largest tree would seem a paltry wand in his hand. In Book III, he disguises himself as a cherub, but his inner turmoil ultimately ruins this benign-seeming appearance. Satan is later described as leaping over Eden's fence like a wolf into a sheep's pen. While he does not exactly take the form of a wolf, he continues to be compared to and associated with wild, predatory animals. He takes the shape of a bird atop the Tree of Life, then morphs into a toad to whisper temptation into Eve's ear. Satan's shapes become progressively less impressive and stately. Once an imposing figure, he shrinks himself to become a lesser angel, then a mere bird, and finally a much less appealing animal: a toad.

In this book, we are presented with Eve's first memories of awakening to consciousness, though we have to wait until Book VIII to see Adam's first memories. Eve's account subtly underscores her distance from God and need for guidance. She awakens in shade rather than daylight, suggesting her separation from the light of God's truth. Almost immediately, she finds herself captivated and deceived by an image—her reflection in the water, which she does not recognize as merely an image. She admits that she would probably still be by the water's edge, fixated there in vain desire, if it wasn't for God's calling her away. This image recalls the story of Narcissus from Ovid's *Metamorphoses,* a story that Renaissance poets such as Petrarch used to show that erotic desire is based on visual images that are inherently vain and deceptive. Milton's allusion to Narcissus makes a similar point: human beings, especially women, need God's help to escape the trap of desire based on images. Significantly, it is the voice rather than the visual image of God that calls her away. Also noteworthy in this context is the fact that in his first speech to Eve, God says that Eve is herself an image—the reflection of Adam.

After God leads Eve away from her reflection, she first encounters Adam under a platan tree. Platan is the Greek name for plane tree, and by giving the name of the tree in Greek rather than English, Milton alludes to Plato, the Greek philosopher, whose name is etymologically linked with that of the plane tree. The most well-known of Plato's arguments is the thesis that reality consists of ideal forms that can only be perceived by the intellect, in contrast with the deceptive shades or reflections of these ideal forms that human beings perceive in everyday life. Milton associates the platan tree, or Plato, with Adam, suggesting that he is closer to the ideal forms or essences of things, whereas Eve is more part of the world of images, shade, and illusion, and is led away from illusions only reluctantly.

Milton's presentation of Adam and Eve was controversial in his time. Milton paints an idyllic picture of an innocent, strong, and intelligent Adam, whereas Christian tradition more typically emphasizes Adam's basically sinful nature. The Puritans, like many other Christians, viewed the sexual act as inherently sinful—a necessary evil that cannot be avoided precisely because man has fallen. Milton, in contrast, makes a point of noting that Adam and Eve enjoy pure, virtuous sexual pleasure without sin: they love, but do not lust. Milton implies that not only is sex not evil, but that demonizing it goes against God's will. He persuasively argues that God mandates procreation, and that anyone who would advocate complete abstinence (as St. Paul does in the New Testament) would be an enemy to God and God's magnificent creation. Furthermore, Eve's story about seeing her reflection in the water hints that her vanity may become a serious flaw—and weakness—later on. Her curiosity is sparked by her lack of understanding about who she is and where she is. She traces the river back to its source just as she wishes to trace herself to her source, through emotional self-reflection, in search of answers to her difficult questions. Also, her willingness to listen and believe the voice she hears, which tells her about her identity, also foreshadows that she will trust another voice she will hear later—Satan's.

Milton's presentation of Adam and Eve is controversial in our own time because the discourse between Adam and Eve strikes many modern audiences as misogynistic. Milton portrays Adam as her superior because he has a closer relationship to God. The idea that Adam was created to serve God only, and Eve is created to serve both God and Adam, illustrates Milton's belief that women were created to serve men. The narrator remarks of Adam and Eve that their difference in quality was apparent—"their sex not equal seemed" (IV.296). Milton implies that she is weaker in mind as well as body than Adam. Eve herself freely admits her secondary and subordinate role. When she explains her dependence on him she explains to Adam that she is created because of him and is lost without him. Having Eve herself possess and verbalize these misogynistic, submissive views adds a peculiar and somewhat disturbing power to the conversation. Milton's views on the relations between men and women were certainly common, if not dogmatic, in his time. Milton's reading of the Bible dictated that in marriage the woman is to obey the man, and that he is her ruler. The relationship between Adam and Eve, though unequal, remains perfectly happy, because they both in the end live in praise of God. Eve accepts her role as Adam does his own, and God loves both equally.

BOOK V

SUMMARY

Adam awakes from a peaceful sleep, but Eve appears to have been restless during the night. She relates to him the disturbing dream she has had. She explains that in the dream she hears a voice and follows it to the Tree of Knowledge. There, a creature who looks like an angel appears, takes a fruit from the forbidden tree and tastes it. The angel tells Eve that she could be like the gods if she eats too, but before she can try it, he vanishes and she returns to dreamless sleep. Adam is troubled by the dream, but assures her that it is not necessarily a prediction of what will happen in the future, because she still has the faculty of reason to control her actions. Comforted, they return to their work and praise of God.

Meanwhile, in Heaven, God calls the Archangel Raphael to his side. He does not want Adam and Eve to claim that the devil took them by surprise if they are lured into disobedience, so he instructs Raphael to tell Adam about the danger in store for him. When Raphael arrives in Paradise, the couple warmly welcomes him. They eat together, and Raphael explains the differences between heavenly food and earthly food. After the meal, Eve leaves the scene and allows Raphael to speak to Adam.

Raphael first describes the composition of the things God created on Earth. God gave different kinds of substance to all living things. The highest substance is spirit, which God put into humankind. Below humans are animals, which have living flesh but no spirit, followed by plants and then inanimate objects. Each group possesses the attributes of the groups below it; for instance, whereas animals have physical senses, humankind possesses all of the same senses plus the ability to reason. Raphael says that man is the highest being on Earth because of his God-given ability to reason, and warns Adam to always choose obedience to God. Adam wonders how any being created by God could choose to be disobedient, but Raphael explains that Adam was created as perfect yet mutable, endowed with the power to maintain his perfection but also the power to lose it. Adam desires to know more, and asks how disobedience first came into Heaven. To answer, Raphael relates the story of Satan's fall.

When Heaven was still at peace, Raphael explains, all the hierarchies of angels were obedient to God. One day the Father announced to them that he had begotten a son, who was to rule at his right hand. While God's announcement pleased most of the angels, one of them was angry. That angry angel lost his heavenly name, and is now called Satan. Proud to be one of the highest archangels, Satan felt that he deserved the same powers as God. Jealous of the Son, he persuaded one third of the other angels in Heaven to join him. Satan erected his own throne in heaven, and told his followers that they should not allow themselves to be unjustly ruled.

One of these followers, however, disagreed. He was named Abdiel, and after arguing with Satan he faithfully returned to the side of God, braving the scorn of the other rebellious angels.

ANALYSIS

Eve's dream, created by Satan's whispering in her ear as she sleeps, foreshadows her ultimate temptation and downfall. God's decision to send Raphael to warn Adam about the dangers ahead also foreshadows their fall, although the fact that it does so is paradoxical. After all, the ostensible purpose of sending Raphael is to arm Adam and Eve with knowledge, so that they won't fall from sheer ignorance. We might expect Raphael's visit to give Adam and Eve a fighting chance, creating more suspense and doubt as to the outcome, but this is not the case. Every Christian reader already knows that Adam and Eve will fall, so instead of creating suspense, Raphael's words of instruction only heighten our sense of the gravity of their sin and the tragedy of their disobedience.

There is a further paradox in the fact that even as Milton foreshadows the fall and makes it seem inevitable and predestined, he strives to prove that the fall was anything but inevitable. *Paradise Lost* insists that Adam and Eve had free will and were protected by adequate knowledge and understanding. In fact, Milton's poem goes much further in this regard than the Bible, which does not include Raphael's warning visit or God's own assurance that Adam and Eve have free will. These parts of the story are Milton's invention, and his insistence on humankind's free will flew in the face of what most Puritans believed. Since we know the end of the story from the first line of the poem, this emphasis on free will does not generate an impression of greater possibility, but rather informs our understanding of what Adam and Eve's sin means.

When Raphael begins to tell Adam about the war in Heaven, he first admits that explaining these events presents a challenge, because the spiritual beings involved are beyond human comprehension, and it may even be unlawful for him to tell of these things. Raphael here describes problems that Milton himself has to confront in *Paradise Lost,* including how to narrate religious mysteries in a form that will be understood, but also the problem of what authorizes Milton to explain these mysteries at all. Much of *Paradise Lost* is based on the Book of Genesis, but much of it is Milton's invention. Moreover, Milton presents his epic not as a fiction based on Christian scripture, but as a divinely inspired Christian document. We may well wonder why Milton, a devout Christian, thought he could presume to explain such matters as the origins of Christ and Satan and the details of life in Paradise. Part of the answer probably is that Milton truly believes that his poem is divinely inspired, and that the Holy Spirit, as the source of all creativity, speaks through him. Another part of the answer may be that Milton does present *Paradise Lost* as a fiction that conveys truths not literally but allegorically. Thus, he adapts his subject matter to the conventional expectations of an epic poem, thereby using a literary form that his audience was already familiar with. The truth of his poem lies in its interpretation rather than in its plot.

One way in which Milton follows the conventions of epic poetry is by having Raphael narrate the long background story of the origin and course of the war in Heaven. The great Greek and Latin epics begin by situating their characters in the middle of the story and then turning backward to recount events that occurred before the story began. This style of narration, referred to as *in medias res* (Latin for "in the middle of things"), allows the epic poem to begin with engaging scenes and action to immediately engage our interest and attention. When the story is underway, the narrator can confidently return to fill in the gaps in our knowledge and give us further context about the story we are reading. Milton uses a similar tactic in Book V, throwing both Adam and us, the readers, in the middle of the story. We, like Adam, have heard only about Heaven's side of the war in Heaven and about Adam and Eve's early days. Raphael then informs us of the world's creation and its structures and hierarchies.

Milton uses Raphael's story to present another of his unorthodox religious views. Milton believed that the Son had an origin and was thus not eternal. This notion challenged traditional Christian belief, which holds that the Son (Jesus) is coeternal with the Father —although they relate as father and son, there was no "birth" or starting point for the divine relationship or for either of them. Since they are two parts of the same eternal God, they must both have existed for eternity. Milton rejects this idea with his assertion that there was a specific time when the Father begat the Son. Milton certainly did not deny the divinity of Jesus, but his challenging belief in Jesus' separate origin reminds us that he was never afraid to distance himself from conventional religion, and that he trusted his own interpretations more than those of any institution.

BOOK VI

SUMMARY

Raphael continues his story of the first conflict between Satan and the Father. Again, Raphael gestures that he must find a way to relate the war in terms that Adam will understand. Raphael returns to his story with Abdiel, who confronts Satan and the other rebel angels and tells them that their defeat is imminent. He leaves the followers of Satan and is welcomed back into the ranks of God. He is forgiven by God and praised for his loyalty, obedience, and resistance of evil. God appoints Gabriel and Michael the leaders of Heaven's army, which is justly made up of only as many angels as Satan's army.

Shortly thereafter, the two sides prepare their armies. The two armies line up in full view of each other, waiting for the signal to attack. Satan and Abdiel square off in the middle; they exchange insults, and then blows, and the battle begins. Both sides fight fiercely and evenly until Michael, the co-leader of the good angels, deals Satan a blow with an unusually large and intimidating sword. The sword slices through Satan's entire right side, and the rebellious angels then retreat with their wounded leader. But because angels have no bodies, says Milton, they can only be wounded temporarily, and Satan is able to regroup for the next day of fighting. Satan easily rouses himself and his followers for a second day of battle arguing that better weapons must yield better results. He plans to use a secret weapon, cannons, which the rebels spend the entire night building.

Satan's army unveils the cannons the next day and bombards the good angels. The good angels find themselves at a disadvantage as their armor becomes a hindrance to their escape. Michael finally provides a solution: the good angels pick up mountains and move them across the battlefield to bury the rebel angels and their artillery. The rebel angels must slowly dig themselves out from underneath the mountains and reassemble. Night falls, and God decides that there will be no fighting on the third day, and that the war must now end. He sends out his Son the next day, who charges through the enemy ranks on a great chariot and drives them from the battlefield. The Son, endowed with the power of God, surrounds the rebel angels, Satan included, and drives them out of the Gate of Heaven through a hole in Heaven's ground. They fall for nine days through Chaos, before landing in Hell.

Raphael warns Adam and Eve that Satan has begun to plot the doom of mankind. Raphael hypothesizes that Satan, in order to get revenge, wishes to make them commit sin to tarnish God's beloved creation. Raphael adds that Satan may also want others to rebel against God and suffer a similar fate. Raphael explains to Adam that they must fear Satan and must not yield to his evil plot.

ANALYSIS

The war in Heaven is probably intended to be read as a metaphor, encapsulating spiritual lessons in an epic scenario so that we (and Adam) can understand what Raphael is talking about. The story certainly contains lessons that Raphael wants Adam to learn from. One of the morals of the war in Heaven is that disobedience leads to a person's becoming blind to the truth. Satan and the rebel angels feel empowered by their new decision not to submit, yet their opposition to God actually renders them powerless. Satan and his army never seem to realize the futility of their rebellion. Satan rouses himself and his troops to more and more disobedience, but their continued failure and continued hope of victory demonstrate the blinding effect that their pride and vanity have wrought. Thus blinded, they are easily overcome in battle each day, by only a small portion of God's angels actually fighting against them. Adam tries to learn the parallel between the battle between good and evil that occurred in Heaven and the battle that will occur subtly on Earth. In similar fashion, we are supposed to envision the parallel of Adam's struggle in our own lives, as we strive to ward off evil and attain virtue.

Raphael's narrative makes the war in Heaven seem unreal, and almost cartoonish. As Raphael explains, angels are exempt from death, which lessens the consequences of the battle and thus makes it seem that less is at stake. Satan, for instance, is grievously wounded by Michael's sword—he is almost hacked in two—but he is ready to fight the next day. The good angels pick up entire mountains and sling them at the rebel angels. Unable to die or even be seriously wounded, the rebel angels can dig themselves out from under the mountainous rubble, dust themselves off, and plan for their next strike. The entire war comes to seem rather silly because it lacks drama. The outcome is never in doubt.

The style of battle does not resemble the warfare of Milton's day, but rather the feudal warfare of earlier epics. Milton presents the warring factions each lining up with their spears and shields across a battlefield. The battlefield discussions between the two sides before battle are reminiscent of scenes in Homer's *Iliad* and Virgil's *Aeneid*. Then, amid classical style warfare, the rebel angels employ what was in Milton's time a relatively new and dangerous weapon of war: a gunpowder cannon. Milton introduces this discrepancy in modes of warfare to allude to his society's advancements over those of the classical age. Satan's invention of the cannon is an unexpected development, signaling Milton's belief that gunpowder is a demonic invention and that so-called advancements in war are futile and worthless.

BOOK VII

SUMMARY

At the halfway point of the twelve books of *Paradise Lost*, Milton once more invokes a muse, but this time it is Urania, the Muse of Astronomy. Milton refers to her in Christian terms, as a source of inspiration much like the Holy Spirit. He asks Urania to insure his safe transition from relating the story of the war in Heaven back to Raphael and Adam's conversation on Earth. Again, Milton asks that the muse inspire him through the rest of Raphael's speech and protect him from the troublesome beliefs of others who do not have access to her wisdom.

Back on Earth, Adam asks Raphael about how and why the world was created, as well as about his own creation. Adam initially believes that he may not be allowed to hear the story of creation, so he asks cautiously, although his curiosity is overwhelming. Raphael agrees to tell him, explaining that the story of creation is not a secret to be kept from human beings. Raphael begins by picking up where he left off, with the fall of Satan and his rebel followers. He explains that shortly after the fall, the Father wished to forge a new race, partly to erase the memory of the rebellion and partly to make up for the rebels' absence from the ranks of God's loyal creations. Raphael believes that by replacing the fallen angels, God renders Satan unable to claim that he diminished God's creation. By creating Earth and mankind in a nearly empty part of the universe, God shows the fallen angels that his glorious kingdom can be expanded indefinitely. For all these reasons, God decides to create Earth and humans, with the idea that Earth and Heaven will eventually be joined together as one kingdom through mankind's obedience to God's divine will.

Raphael says that God sends the Son down into Chaos to create Earth. The Earth is first formed out of Chaos and given light and dark, or night and day, in equal measure. Land is separated from water, and animals are created to populate both land and sea. The creation takes six days, and Adam and Eve are created last. The entire act of creation is done through the Son, who makes man in his image and gives him authority over all the animals on Earth. God gives Adam one command: he must not eat the fruit from the Tree of Knowledge, which gives knowledge of good and evil. The Son, finishing with his work, hangs Earth beneath Heaven by a chain. He reascends to Heaven as the angels sing hymns and praise his work. Pleased with his work, God rests on the seventh day, which then becomes known as the Sabbath.

ANALYSIS

In the same manner as the two previous invocations of the muse, Milton's invocation of Urania fuses classical allusion with Christian belief. Milton reconfigures Urania and likens her to the Holy Spirit, placing a corrective, Christian spin on an old mythological figure. The cumulative effect of Milton's allusions to and corrections of classical culture is to convey the impression that Greek and Roman civilization was indeed great, but misled in its philosophy and religion. Thus Milton can claim to build upon the achievements of classical authors while replacing their religious beliefs with Christian ones. Being born before Christ, most classical authors do have a good excuse for not professing Christian beliefs. In this respect, Milton's stance toward antiquity is not unlike that of earlier Christian poets such as Dante or Spenser, who were similarly steeped in classical literary culture.

Raphael's account of the world's creation closely follows the biblical account of creation in the first few chapters of Genesis. Milton takes some of his language directly from popular English translations of the Bible. By using biblical language, Milton gives Raphael's account more authority and renders the invented details of his story more credible as well. Raphael's extended explanations about the world and about God and Satan are lengthy, but their length demonstrates Milton's beliefs concerning the absolute importance of conversation, knowledge, and thought. Book VII presents a curious Adam who seeks knowledge and an agreeable Raphael who disposes his knowledge in human terms. Their evolving interaction in this book differs from their interaction in earlier books, as Adam becomes more aggressive in his attempts to gain wisdom from Raphael. Throughout their conversation, the desire for knowledge is expressed through metaphors of hunger, eating, and digestion. Adam's craving for knowledge begins to surface in this book and foreshadows his potential temptation to eat from the Tree of Knowledge.

The Son is given a more significant role in Book VII than he has in previous books, illustrating that he is the instrument through which God acts. Milton actually departs from the Bible in having the Son create the world, as Genesis says nothing about the Son. But according to Christian teaching, God and the Son are manifestations of the same entity. Milton begins with the orthodox Christian premise of a three-part God and then elaborates on the relationship between God the Father and God the Son. By having God send the Son to defeat Satan and create the universe, Milton shows how God and the Son can work separately yet still work as one God. Even though they appear as separate characters, Milton believed that the Son represents the living, active, almost human likeness of God.

Book VIII

Summary
After Raphael finishes the story of creation, Adam asks him about the motions of the stars, sun, and planets. Eve decides to leave them alone to converse, not because she is bored or unable to grasp the discussion, but because she prefers to hear about the conversation afterward from Adam. Adam assumes from his observations that the other planets orbit the earth, but Raphael explains how it is possible (though not certain) that it only appears this way because of the turning of the Earth on its axis. Raphael mentions to Adam that it does not matter whether the Earth moves or the universe moves around the Earth. Such broad questions often have no possible answers, he explains, because God does not intend human beings to comprehend everything about his creation. Furthermore, Raphael warns Adam that he should be satisfied with the knowledge that God has made available and to resist the urge to gain further understanding outside of the limits he has set.

After listening to Raphael, Adam tells him what he knows about his own creation. He remembers first awakening to consciousness, wondering who and where he was. He quickly realized that he could walk, run, jump, and even speak. Then God came to him and explained how and why he was created, giving him dominion over all the rest of creation, and asking in return only that he not eat from the Tree of Knowledge. Adam surveyed his environment and met the animals of Earth in pairs of two. He had never seen these creatures before, but when God asked him to name the animals, he realized that he already knew each of their names, as God had given him this knowledge beforehand. Adam explains that he soon longed for a companion more equal to himself than the animals, a person with whom he could share his thoughts. To fulfill Adam's desire, God created Eve from a rib in Adam's side while he slept. Adam remembers this fact because God allowed his mind to remain aware of what was happening even while he slept. Upon seeing Eve, Adam fell instantly in love.

Raphael talks to Adam about love, recommending that he refrain from carnal passion and search for a pure love that rejuvenates and expands his mind and body. Yet Adam is worried about his physical attraction to Eve, since she is noticeably less pure than he. Raphael says that while Eve is more beautiful on the outside, she is less worthy than Adam on the inside. Her spirituality is weaker than Adam's, her intellect is slightly less developed, and her vanity is a serious weakness. Raphael tells Adam that his love for Eve must transcend her sexual attractiveness. Adam responds by admitting his physical attraction to Eve while asserting that his love comes from her emotional and spiritual companionship. Raphael reiterates to Adam the danger that he faces with Eve and the need for both of them to avoid Satan's temptations. Afterward, Raphael takes his leave to return to Heaven and Adam goes to sleep.

ANALYSIS

Adam's memory of first awakening to consciousness presents significant differences from Eve's first memories, which we see in Book IV. Whereas Eve awakens in shade, Adam does so in broad sunlight — "happy Light," as he calls it (VIII.285). Eve is quickly drawn in by reflections and images, coming to desire an illusion of herself, and only gradually drawn by God toward Adam and the wisdom represented by the platan tree. Adam, in contrast, looks toward the sky and toward God immediately upon waking up. He quickly discovers that he knows the true names of things, so he is not deceived by mere appearances and shadows. God appears to him as a visible presence rather than merely a voice, and entrusts Adam with his commandments, all of which suggests that Adam is closer to God and to the truth than Eve. When God asks Adam why he wants a companion, given that God himself is solitary and without peer, Adam shows that he understands his own nature, arguing that he is deficient and defective, unlike God.

Adam's account of his first meeting with Eve is somewhat different from the version Eve gives in Book IV. There, Eve says that she turned away from Adam at first because he did not seem as attractive as her own reflection. Although Adam has heard Eve's explanation, in his explanation to Raphael he says that her turning away from him seemed to him to be intentionally designed to make her more attractive to him (whether the intention was Eve's or God's), as it is natural for him to pursue her rather than the other way around. This discrepancy could point to Adam's tendency to deceive himself where Eve is concerned.

Adam and Raphael's description of Eve illustrates Milton's view of the inequality of men and women. Eve's decision to leave Raphael and Adam alone, preferring to hear the conversation from Adam afterward, demonstrates her submission to Adam and her reluctance to converse with the angel herself. We get the sense that she withdraws because she acknowledges her place in God's hierarchy. Moreover, Milton tells us that she prefers to hear the story mingled with Adam's caresses, indicating that intellectual stimulation by itself is not sufficient for her. Her absence allows Adam and Raphael to discuss her openly, but it also implies Milton's belief that women are either uninterested or mentally ill-equipped for intellectual pursuits. Whatever the reason, Eve's lack of knowledge or engagement with reason allows her to remain ignorant to the dangers that lie ahead for her and Adam.

Raphael's account of our solar system displays Milton's knowledge of the conflicting scientific theories and beliefs of his time. Milton was well aware that the organization of the universe was hotly disputed. Some astronomers thought that the universe revolved around the Earth, and others, including Milton's contemporary Galileo (to whom he alludes by name in Book I), felt that the Earth revolved around the sun. While Galileo's theory was widely denounced by religious authorities, Milton does not take either side of the issue in *Paradise Lost*, having Raphael assert that the debate is unimportant because it concerns matters that do not pertain to humankind's relationship with God.

Similarly, Raphael's message to Adam about the limits of human knowledge functions as a warning to scientists in Milton's time.

Many believed that science could yield incorrect and misleading answers to questions about the universe. Milton argues that humankind should resist making theories about the universe and other incomprehensible things, and focus rather on pragmatic issues of their daily spiritual lives. Milton believed in the necessity of scientific questionings and pursuits, but he also believed that the pursuit of truth through science would yield dangerous results. Truth, according to Milton, should only be pursued through faith and religion; humans should tend to their more Earthly practical matters and have faith that God will manage the metaphysical matters of the universe.

Book IX, Lines 1–403

Summary

With Raphael's departure for Heaven, the story no longer consists of conversations between heavenly beings and humankind. Milton explains that he must now turn to Adam and Eve's actual act of disobedience. The poem must now turn tragic, and Milton asserts his intention to show that the fall of humankind is more heroic than the tales of Virgil and Homer. He invokes Urania, the "Celestial Patroness" (IX.21) and muse of Christian inspiration, and asks for her to visit him in his sleep and inspire his words, because he fears he is too old and lacks the creative powers to accomplish the task himself. He hopes not to get caught up in the description of unimportant items, as Virgil and Homer did, and to remain focused on his ultimate and divine task.

Satan returns to the Garden of Eden the night after Raphael's departure. Satan's return comes eight days after he was caught and banished by Gabriel. He sneaks in over the wall, avoiding Gabriel and the other guards. After studying all the animals of the Garden, Satan considers what disguise he should assume, and chooses to become a snake. Before he can continue, however, he again hesitates—not because of doubt this time, but because of his grief at not being able to enjoy this wondrous new world. He struggles to control his thoughts. He now believes that the Earth is more beautiful than Heaven ever was, and becomes jealous of Adam and Eve and their chosen status to occupy and maintain Paradise. He gripes that the excess beauty of Earth causes him to feel more torment and anguish. Gathering his thoughts into action, he finds a sleeping serpent and enters its body.

The next morning, Adam and Eve prepare for their usual morning labors. Realizing that they have much work to do, Eve suggests that they work separately, so that they might get more work done. Adam is not keen on this idea. He fears that they will be more susceptible to Satan's temptation if they are alone. Eve, however, is eager to have her strength tested. After much resistance, Adam concedes, as Eve promises Adam that she will return to their bower soon. They go off to do their gardening independently.

ANALYSIS

Milton begins Book IX as he began Books I and VII: with an invocation and plea for guidance, as well as a comparison of his task to that of the great Greek and Roman epics, the *Iliad*, *Odyssey*, and the *Aeneid*. Milton explains by way of this invocation that Adam and Eve's fall is the major event that occurs in *Paradise Lost*. Their fall is the poem's climax, even though it comes as no surprise. By describing the fall as tragic, Milton conveys the gravity and seriousness of this catastrophe for all of humankind, but he also situates Adam and Eve's story within the literary conventions of tragedy, in which a great man falls because of a special flaw within his otherwise larger-than-life character. The fall paves the way for humankind's ultimate redemption and salvation, and thus Milton can claim that his epic surpasses Homer's and Virgil's because it pertains to the entire human race, not one hero or even one nation.

Milton mocks the knightly romances of the Middle Ages on the grounds that they applaud merely superficial heroism. The idea of the chivalrous warrior was an oxymoron in Milton's view. Milton presents his hero as a morally powerful person—Adam's strength and martial prowess are entirely irrelevant. Milton voices doubts about whether his society will appreciate a real Christian hero, or whether he himself is still skilled enough or young enough to complete his literary task, balancing his confidence in his own ability with the humility appropriate to a Christian poet.

Satan's return to the story presents him as a changed and further degenerated character. Before the temptation of Eve, we see Satan go through another bit of soul-searching. This time, however, he does not waver in his determination to ruin humankind, but only makes a cold expression of regret for things that might have been. Milton notes that Satan is driven to action by the grief and turmoil he feels inside and by his wounded sense of pride. It is clear now that Satan's decision to corrupt humankind is final, yet he still thinks about how he would have enjoyed the beauty of Earth if he had not rebelled. Milton displays the internal agony that results from the sin of despair: Satan can clearly see, despite all his previous arguments, that it would have been better to remain good. However, he has forbidden himself from even considering the possibility of repentance. As a result, he degenerates further and further, making his mind and body his own personal Hell.

Milton has given absolute power to the reason and free will of both men and Satan, only to show that the mind can defeat itself—using reason to arrive at an unreasonable position. Satan's thoughts are increasingly contradictory and confusing, becoming hard for us, and perhaps for himself, to follow. Satan comes to believe his own faulty logic and his own lies. In Books I and II, his ability to reason is strong, but now in Book IX he can hardly form a coherent argument. Ironically, Satan has proved the truth of his own earlier statement that the mind can make a heaven of hell or a hell of heaven. Satan intended to make a heaven out of Hell, where he would be an evil version of God. Instead, he has brought his torture with him, and made a hell out of the earth that, but for him, would be heavenly.

Book IX, Lines 404–1189

Summary

Satan, in the form of the serpent, searches for the couple. He is delighted to find Eve alone. Coiling up, he gets her attention, and begins flattering her beauty, grace, and godliness. Eve is amazed to see a creature of the Garden speak. He tells her in enticing language that he gained the gifts of speech and intellect by eating the savory fruit of one of the trees in the garden. He flatters Eve by saying that eating the apple also made him seek her out in order to worship her beauty.

Eve is amazed by the power that this fruit supposedly gives the snake. Curious to know which tree holds this fruit, Eve follows Satan until he brings her to the Tree of Knowledge. She recoils, telling him that God has forbidden them to eat from this tree, but Satan persists, arguing that God actually wants them to eat from the tree. Satan says that God forbids it only because he wants them to show their independence. Eve is now seriously tempted. The flattery has made her desire to know more. She reasons that God claimed that eating from this tree meant death, but the serpent ate (or so he claims) and not only does he still live, but can speak and think. God would have no reason to forbid the fruit unless it were powerful, Eve thinks, and seeing it right before her eyes makes all of the warnings seem exaggerated. It looks so perfect to Eve. She reaches for an apple, plucks it from the tree, and takes a bite. The Earth then feels wounded and nature sighs in woe, for with this act, humankind has fallen.

Eve's first fallen thought is to find Adam and to have him eat of the forbidden fruit too so that they might be equal. She finds him nearby, and in hurried words tells him that she has eaten the fruit, and that her eyes have been opened. Adam drops the wreath of flowers he made for her. He is horrified because he knows that they are now doomed, but immediately decides that he cannot possibly live without Eve. Eve does not want Adam to remain and have another woman; she wants him to suffer the same fate as she. Adam realizes that if she is to be doomed, then he must follow. He eats the fruit. He too feels invigorated at first. He turns a lustful eye on Eve, and they run off into the woods for sexual play.

Adam and Eve fall asleep briefly, but upon awakening they see the world in a new way. They recognize their sin, and realize that they have lost Paradise. At first, Adam and Eve both believe that they will gain glorious amounts of knowledge, but the knowledge that they gained by eating the apple was only of the good that they had lost and the evil that they had brought upon themselves. They now see each other's nakedness and are filled with shame. They cover themselves with leaves. Milton explains that their appetite for knowledge has been fulfilled, and their hunger for God has been quenched. Angry and confused, they continue to blame each other for committing the sin, while neither will admit any fault. Their shameful and tearful argument continues for hours.

ANALYSIS

The ease with which Satan persuades Eve to sin paints an unflattering portrayal of woman, one that accords with Milton's portrayal throughout the poem of women as the weaker sex. Eve allows the serpent's compliments to win her over, demonstrating that she cares more about superficial things such as beauty than profound things such as God's grace. Furthermore, that Eve gives in to the serpent after only a few deceptive arguments reveals her inability to reason soundly. Not only is she herself corruptible, however, but she also seeks to corrupt others: her immediate reaction upon discovering her sin is to lure Adam into her fate. Rather than repent and take full responsibility for her actions, she moves instinctively to drag Adam down with her to make him share her suffering. Eve thus comes across as an immoral and harmful being, one whose values are skewed and who has a bad influence on others.

Satan's argument that knowledge is good because knowing what is good and evil makes it easier to do what is good wrongfully assumes that knowledge is always good. This flaw in his argument is the theological thrust of this book: though the intellect is powerful and god-like, obeying God is a higher priority than feeding the intellect. Milton believes that one cannot first obey reason and then obey God; rather one must trust God and then trust reason. Raphael's wise argument from Book VIII about the limitations of human knowledge and the need to feel comfortable with this limited knowledge, is blatantly neglected or forgotten. If Eve had stayed to listen to Raphael and Adam's discussion and had recognized the dangers of working separately, then she could have been safer from Satan's temptation. Or if Adam had relayed Raphael's warning message to Eve more thoroughly and persuasively, and if he had denied Eve's suggestion that they work separately, then the fall might have been avoidable. Eve overestimates the powers of her ability to protect herself and to resist temptation, and Adam underestimates the need to protect Eve and share his knowledge with her. Both must suffer from each other's shortfalls.

Adam sins not out of a desire to gain the knowledge from eating the fruit, but out of recognition that Eve has left him with little or no alternative. Adam needs even less persuading than Eve to eat the apple, and does so knowing that he is disobeying God. He knows that he could not be happy if Eve were banished, and his desire to stay with Eve overwhelms his desire to obey God. Adam's sin of temptation is choosing Eve over God, letting physical and emotional impulses overtake reason. The wreath of flowers he makes for Eve symbolizes his love for her. When he sees that she has eaten from the Tree of Knowledge, he drops the wreath, symbolizing her fallen state. The dropping of the wreath may also hint at Adam's disappointment in Eve as a spiritual lover and companion, and even his falling out of pure love with her. After Adam eats from the apple, his attraction to Eve changes subtly, and he looks at her more like a connoisseur, eager to indulge. The sexuality the two display is now perverted, their love in the dark forest more lustful and animal-like than their earlier love in the lush, bright bower. Their arguing and blaming of each other demonstrate their lack of unity and peace, and demonstrate, as does the Earth's sighing, their fallen state.

BOOK X

SUMMARY

The scene returns to Heaven, where God knows immediately that Adam and Eve have eaten from the Tree of Knowledge. Gabriel and the other angels guarding Paradise also know, and they fly back up to Heaven. They report that they did all they could to prevent Satan from re-entering the Garden. God tells them that he allowed it himself without condoning it, and acquits his angels of any guilt. He then sends his Son down to Earth to pass judgment on the couple.

In Paradise, the Son calls to Adam, who comes forth shamefacedly along with Eve. They are embarrassed by their nakedness. Asked if they have eaten from the tree, Adam admits that Eve gave the fruit to him to eat, and Eve blames the serpent for persuading her to take it. The Son first condemns the serpent, whose body Satan possessed to tempt Eve. He ordains that all snakes now must crawl on their bellies, never to carry themselves upright again. The Son decrees that Adam and Eve's children will bruise the serpent's head, while serpent will forever bite humans by the heel. As punishment for the couple, Eve and all women to follow will give birth in pain, and must submit to their husbands. Likewise, Adam and all men after him will have to labor to hunt and harvest food in cursed ground. After passing these sentences, the Son returns to Heaven.

Meanwhile in Hell, Sin and Death remain at the gate of Hell where Satan left them. Sensing that Satan has succeeded in his task, they finish the bridge linking Hell to Earth and begin to travel toward Earth to meet him. At the edge of Paradise, Sin and Death meet Satan. They congratulate him for succeeding in his mission and promise him that they will infect the Earth. Death will corrupt all living things, causing them to die, and Sin will corrupt the thoughts and deeds of humankind. They also tell Satan that his success must have allowed them to leave Hell, proving that he has established his control over humankind and Earth. Satan thanks Sin and Death for their praises and urges them to hurry on their way to conquer Earth. Satan believes that he has in fact acquired the special powers Sin and Death spoke of, when in truth God allows them to enter Earth so that the Son can conquer them when he becomes human. Now, Satan goes back down to Hell, where his followers have been eagerly waiting his return. Satan speaks to them from Pandemonium, tells them of his triumph, and expects to hear riotous applause. Instead, he hears hisses signifying scorn for him and his devastating act. The devils have all been transformed into snakes, along with Satan, who did not understand the punishment the Son foretold. A grove of trees appears in Hell, with fruit that turns to ashes as soon as the snakes try to bite it.

Sin and Death arrive on Earth and begin their work. From Heaven, God sees that they have come to Earth and tells his angels that he will allow Sin and Death to stay on Earth until Judgement Day. After then, they must return to Hell and be forever locked up with Satan and the other devils.

God now calls for his angels to alter the universe. They tilt the Earth's axis or alter the path of the sun (the poem allows for both interpretations). Now humankind will have to endure extreme hot and cold seasons, instead of enjoying the constant temperate climate that existed before Adam and Eve's fall from God's grace. Meanwhile, Discord follows Sin to Earth and causes animals to war with each other and with humans too. Seeing these changes, Adam is sorrowful, and laments. He knows that the rest of humankind will suffer because of his disobedience, and wishes that he could bear all of the punishment upon himself. He curses life and wishes that Death would come at once to alleviate his misery. Instead, Eve comes to him. But Adam is angry; he blames and insults Eve's female nature, wondering why God ever created her. She begs his forgiveness, and pleads with him not to leave her. She reminds him that the snake tricked her, but she fully accepts the blame for sinning against both God and him. She argues that unity and love can save them in a fallen world. She longs for death and suggests that they take their own lives, but Adam forbids it. Eve's speech affects Adam. He becomes calm, consoling her and sharing responsibility for their fall. They must stop blaming each other, he says. They must live with their mistakes and make the most out of their fallen state. Remembering the prophecy that Eve's seed would bruise the head of the serpent, he feels that there is hope for humankind and advises that they obey God and implore his mercy and forgiveness. They return to the spot where they were punished. There, they fall to their knees, confess their sins, and ask for forgiveness.

SUMMARY & ANALYSIS

ANALYSIS

If Book IX presents the climax of *Paradise Lost,* then Book X presents its resolution, as the punishments that the Son hands out restore some sort of order to the world. Satan and the other supporting characters disappear from the rest of the poem, eliminating the source of human temptation and thus focusing the poem on Adam and Eve's regret. But Adam and Eve begin to redeem humankind with their repentance at the end of Book X. As a result, these characters will disappear from the story, and humankind's predicted redemption will take precedence as the story continues, with Adam and Eve learning about their fallen future.

The devils' punishment to live as snakes forever tempted by fruit on a glorious tree echoes Satan's temptation of Eve. Now they must forever suffer the pains of desire without ever having hope of attaining their wishes, a punishment befitting their crime. To have the devils frozen in a state of perpetual desire and unattainable satisfaction is fit for a group of evildoers who continue to battle God through their disobedience.

Milton uses the concept of typology—the Christian belief that Old Testament characters symbolize and predict New Testament characters—to demonstrate the intimate relationship between the fall of humankind and the redemption of humankind. This relationship between the fall and the resurrection forms the base of the Christian interpretation of the Bible. Milton considers Mary, the mother of the Son (Jesus), to be the "second Eve." As Sin and Death came into the world through Eve, the Son would conquer Sin and Death through Mary. Likewise, Milton considers Jesus to be a "second Adam" who corrects Adam and Eve's disobedience through his resurrection. Through these comparisons between Eve and Mary, and Adam and Jesus, the fall and the resurrection become intertwined. The fall is the cause of human history; the resurrection is the result of human history.

Although Adam and Eve are ailing at the end of Book IX, they take action in Book X and separate their fate from Satan's fate. Satan, as Milton shows, cannot allow himself to repent. His damnation is permanent since his disobedience comes from within and without repentance. On the other hand, humankind's disobedience comes from the temptation of another. This idea helps to explain Adam and Eve's actions and subsequent punishment at the end of Book X. Realizing the terrible consequences of their actions, they come dangerously close to rationalizing suicide, but Adam decides to beg God for forgiveness—the only right answer, in Milton's opinion. Though the coming of the Son and the salvation of humankind had already been foretold, the couple's decision to repent is crucial in God's willingness to forgive them. God will show mercy when asked, but as we see with Satan, there can be no mercy without repentance. In one of the most important quotations in *Paradise Lost,* Milton poetically demonstrates the importance of Adam and Eve's decision in the last several lines of Book X. Adam explains how their repentance and prayer will occur, and then as they pray, Milton duplicates Adam's explanation as the actual action of their prayer. As Adam explains to Eve:

> What better can we do, than to the place
> Repairing where he judg'd us, prostrate fall
> Before him reverent, and there confess
> Humbly our faults, and pardon beg, with tears
> Watering the ground... (XI.1087–1090)

This moment of prayer is crucial because now humankind will not all go the way of Satan, because man produces what the devil could not: true sorrow and regret.

Milton gives Eve the ability to argue persuasively to Adam, showing her intelligence and talents after all. Eve's displays a new humility and grace when she repents after the fall. Her strength lies in her ability to relate her feelings to Adam, feelings that Adam shares. Eve's contemplation of suicide is a sign of weakness, but after Eve's moving speech, Adam is able to help see—and to help her see—why they should not commit suicide. As they lose hope of Paradise, they witness the hope of their race: God's Son, Jesus. It is this hope that prevents the couple from taking their own lives when they realize the extent of their punishment. They choose hope over despair. Milton resolves their distinguished differences through a display of unity: Eve's loving and emotional arguments to stay together and Adam's rational argument to repent help them begin to save humankind together. Their similarities and teamwork, not their differences and occasional parity, allow them to obey reason and survive.

SUMMARY & ANALYSIS

BOOK XI

SUMMARY

God hears the prayers of Adam and Eve, inspired by his own grace. He allows his Son to act as an advocate for humankind, and eventually pay for humankind's sins. The Father then calls all the angels of Heaven together, and announces his plans. He commands the Archangel Michael to go down to Earth and escort Adam and Eve out of Paradise. They can no longer live in a pure place now that they are impure. But through leading a good and moral life, they may be reunited with God after their death. To make the news easier on them, God allows Michael to show Adam a vision of what is to come in the future of humankind.

Adam anticipates that God has heard their prayers. He reassures Eve that she will be able to seek revenge on Satan by being the mother of humankind. She still feels ashamed for bringing Sin and Death into the world, and does not feel that she deserves to have such a role. Nevertheless, she asserts, she will try to obey God and live peacefully in Paradise. Michael then flies down from Heaven and tells them that they must leave Paradise. This news shocks and saddens them, even though their death will be delayed so that they may live for many years. Michael comforts them with the knowledge that all of the Earth, not just Paradise, has been given to them by God and is under the eye of the Father. They are saddened to leave Paradise but know they must obey God's command. Adam laments that he will never be able to speak with God again, but Michael explains that Adam can speak to God wherever he goes. The Archangel then puts Eve to sleep and takes Adam up to a high hill to show him visions of humankind's future.

From the highest hill in Paradise, Michael allows Adam to see nearly an entire hemisphere of the Earth. Adam sees two men offering sacrifices, and watches in horror as one of them kills the other. Michael explains that these men are Cain and Abel, the first sons of Adam and Eve. Adam is shocked and dismayed at his first vision of death. The angel then shows him the other ways that death will take the lives of men: disease, war, and old age. Adam asks if there is any alternative to death, woefully declaring that he could not die too soon, but Michael advises him that obeying God and living a virtuous life can allow people to live long and fruitful lives, so long as Heaven permits.

Next a vision appears of men and women enjoying dances, games, and amorous courting. Adam assumes that this vision is a good portent, but Michael informs him that they are atheists who live for pleasure, not for God, and that they will die as well. This image is followed by the appearance of great armies, slaughtering men by the thousands and plundering cities. Michael tells how war will be praised by violent men, and many terrible conquerors will be admired as heroes. One man, Michael explains, will try to prevent these wars: Enoch. The other men shun him and threaten to kill him, until God lifts him up and brings him safely to Heaven. The scene then changes to further sins of death and dancing and sex. These scenes depict a later era in which sins of the flesh will abound. A single man can be seen, preaching to the others to repent and stop this evil way of life, but he is ignored. He goes off into the mountains and constructs a giant boat, filling it with all the animals of the Earth, and his family. A great flood then comes, wiping out all living things except those on the boat. The good man who builds the boat is Noah. Michael explains how God was angered by humankind's sinful ways, and decided to cleanse the earth of them. He finds one virtuous man, Noah, and preserves humankind through him. The flood wipes out all human life except for Noah and his family. At the end of the flood, Adam sees a rainbow appear and God's covenant with humankind that he will never again destroy the Earth by flood. Adam feels reassured by this story and its promise that virtue and obedience to God will continue on Earth through Noah.

ANALYSIS

The visions in Books XI and XII provide a larger context to *Paradise Lost* and allow Milton to "justify the ways of God to men" (I.26) and to conclude his epic poem with the message that one must live virtuously and be obedient to God. These stories, narrated as Adam's visions, explain why God allows sin and death into the world, and why God wants us to live a certain way. Without these visions and stories, Milton could not explain God's reasoning and his glorious plan for humankind. These visions enable Milton to transcend his focus from the first narrative in the Bible to subsequent books, so that he can discuss human history in broad terms. Part of his message is that human history should be told in terms of its sins, not its advancements in civilizations or invention. These visions expose a dangerous cycle of sins, from sloth and envy to gluttony and lust. Through these visions, Milton asserts the need for repentance and service to God.

Adam and Eve's repentance is made possible through the grace of God. The act of repentance was necessary for salvation, and since God wanted humankind to be redeemed, he planted the seeds of repentance in the souls of Adam and Eve. This realization is appropriate to the belief that humankind, after the fall, is totally depraved. Adam and Eve cannot do anything good on their own accord without God's guidance. God also now specifically reveals why he allows Death to come into the world. Humankind is now impure and unfit for Paradise, as well as for the kingdom of Heaven. The sacrifice of Jesus makes humankind worthy of Heaven: his sacrifice is humankind's final remedy. The price of Jesus' sacrifice is heavy, but the reward outweighs the cost. After death, humankind can be purified and renewed, thus restoring them to their previous position as God's obedient children.

The whole sequence of visions contains a careful emotional balance between grief at the corruption of sin and joy at the redemption of the moral soul. Michael evokes this balance through these visions to inform Adam of humankind's sins and punishments, as well as their sacrifices and rewards. Otherwise, he might have given up hope, and God does not want humankind to fall victim to the same despair that doomed Satan. On the other hand, Adam cannot fail to realize just how depraved humankind will become as a result of the fall—Adam and Eve's sins will be repeated again and again by their children and their children's children. The vision of ensuing decay through war, disease and intemperate living gives Adam a tremendous sense of worry and shame. But the figure of Enoch, the one who is saved by God, demonstrates the need to stand up for one's moral beliefs, even if other nonbelievers will kill one for such integrity. The strength and hope in Enoch's story gives Adam the confidence he needs to continue living obedient to God.

Milton presents Adam, along with other men from his vision, as prefigurations of Christ. The whole scene with Adam on the mountain prefigures an event in Jesus' life. In the Gospels, Satan takes Jesus up onto a mountain and offers him all the kingdoms of the world, if he will bow down in worship to the devil. Adam's time on the mountain is not such a test, but it does tax his courage. Likewise, Enoch's ability to stand up for his beliefs shows the redemptive qualities of humankind. The story of Noah shows that his unwavering belief in God helps to save the virtues of humankind. Noah is given such an important place here because Milton, like many other Christian thinkers, thought of him as a Christ figure: a single man whose virtue in the face of evil saves humankind. From the stories of Enoch and Noah, Adam can recognize the power of devotion to God. These visions, and Adam himself, demonstrate the path of greatness that prefigures the salvation of humankind through Jesus' sacrifice. These visions also demonstrate Milton's belief that a true measure of a person, from Adam up until modern times, is his or her virtuous relationship with God.

BOOK XII

SUMMARY

Michael continues relating the story of the future of humankind to Adam. After the flood, humankind develops from a "second stock": Noah and his family (XII.7). Humans now act more obediently to God than humans before the Flood, offering sacrifices from their flocks and fields. However, several generations later, a leader arrives with proud and ungodly ambitions. This upstart is Nimrod, a tyrant who forces many men under his rule. He constructs the Tower of Babel in an attempt to reach up to Heaven. As punishment, God decrees that men will now speak different languages and be unable to understand each other. Adam agrees with Michael that no one should have dominion over other people, who are by nature free. Michael qualifies this freedom: because of the fall, he says, men only have true liberty when they obey "right reason," or reason tempered by conscience (XII.84). Still, Michael adds, it remains a great sin for one person to take away the liberty of another.

Continuing his story, Michael explains that God chooses Israel as the one nation to rise above the rest. He takes one person, Abraham, father of the Israelites, from a race that worships idols. At God's command, Abraham sets off from his native land and travels to Canaan, the Promised Land. His descendants eventually move to Egypt, and become enslaved by Pharaoh, the ruler of Egypt. Finally, a man named Moses is born, and he eventually leads the people out of Egypt, through the plagues brought down upon the Pharaoh. Michael tells how God allowed the Israelites to pass through the Red Sea, then closed the waters around the Pharaoh's army, which had come to recapture the Israelites. The followers of Moses must travel through the desert to return to Canaan, but they survive with the help of God.

Adam is much relieved to hear that God will bless a portion of humankind, after having it cursed for so long. But he does not understand how all the laws given to these people can possibly be obeyed, or how the Israelites are to remain just before God. Michael replies that they cannot remain just, even if they obey the law, until a greater sacrifice is made. He explains that after generations, the Israelites will turn more and more to sin, until God decides to strengthen their enemies. When they repent, God will save them from these same enemies. After many different rulers, there will come a king named David, and from his descendants will eventually come a Messiah, or chosen one. This Messiah, also known as Jesus or the Son, will once again bring together Earth and Heaven. However, he will have to suffer for it: he shall be hated by many while he lives and will be distrusted, betrayed, and punished by death. However, the grave will not hold this Messiah for long, and rising up he will defeat both Sin and Death, and bruise the head of Satan. His resurrection fulfills the prophecy about the Son finally punishing Satan through his sacrifice. Adam worries that the followers of Jesus will be persecuted, and Michael confirms that they will indeed be persecuted. However, the Archangel says, from Heaven the Messiah will send down the Holy Spirit to provide spiritual protection. But after the first followers die, corrupt leaders as well as good ones will enter the church. Thus those who genuinely follow the truth will still be prosecuted, laments Michael: the world will continue to accommodate evil and make it difficult for individuals to do good deeds. Finally, the Messiah will return a second time, to judge all humankind and reunite Heaven and Earth.

Adam is now more than comforted. He can hardly believe that out of his evil deed so much good will come. Now, however, it is time for him and Eve to leave Paradise. He comes down from the mountain with Michael. Eve awakens from her sleep and tells Adam that she has had an educating dream. Michael then leads the couple to the gate of Eden. There he stands with other angels, brandishing a sword of flame that will forever protect the entrance to Paradise. Slowly and tearfully, Adam and Eve turn away hand in hand with Michael, and wander out into a new world.

ANALYSIS

The discussion between Adam and Michael about Nimrod and the Tower of Babel provides Milton with an opportunity to express his fundamental ideas about political and religious freedom. Adam's admonishment of Nimrod for trying to control other men is the most extreme example of Milton's distrust of institutions and his absolute faith in the ability of the individual person to make his own decisions. Humankind's freedom has already been restricted by the fall, but humankind can still obey reason if individuals think and act separately and for God. When individuals use reason in this way, then they possess true freedom. However, because of Adam's sin, humankind will find it difficult to always follow reason; when an individual strays from God and from reason, he becomes a slave to passions and desires, and is thus not truly free at all, but becomes a slave to desire. This paradox is the reason why Milton did not feel that total individual freedom, within the Church for example, would result in anarchy. Each person can act separately with reason and obey God. The rest of Michael's discourse follows the biblical accounts closely. He progresses through the Old Testament, working his way through the most significant events until he comes to the line of King David, the line from which the Messiah would come. When Milton comes to Jesus' birth, he works more of his own personal interpretations into the biblical story. When Adam asks Michael how the Israelites could possibly follow all of the laws that God gave them, which are contained in the four books following Genesis in the Bible, Milton begins a brief discussion of the Christian view of Old Testament law. Through the vision, Milton explains that law can identify and punish wrongdoing but cannot abolish or eradicate it completely. Without a proper remedy for Adam's sin, attempts to obey God's law only emphasize humankind's sinfulness, according to Christian belief. This lack of a remedy is why the Israelites failed time and again to keep their covenant with God. When a worthy sacrifice is made, when Jesus offers himself on the cross, only then could humankind be capable of doing anything pleasing to God.

Adam brings up the pivotal concept of the fortunate fall, which asserts that the fall of humankind is fortunate for several reasons. Adam and Eve's disobedience allows God to show his mercy and temperance in their punishments and his eternal providence toward humankind. This display of love and compassion, given through the Son, is a gift to humankind. Humankind must now experience pain and death, but it can also experience mercy, salvation, and grace in ways it would not have been able to had Adam and Eve not disobeyed. While humankind has fallen from grace, it can redeem and save itself through a continued devotion and obedience to God. The salvation of humankind, in the form of the Son's (Jesus') sacrifice and resurrection, can begin to restore humankind to its former state. In other words, good will come of sin and death, and humankind will eventually be rewarded. This fortunate result justifies God's reasoning and explains his ultimate plan for humankind.

Adam's ability to perceive the fall as a fortunate one is an inherent paradox in Milton's mixture of the human and the divine. Adam is to be judged according to what he did in his own time, and yet he is allowed to see all the future consequences of his actions in an instant. A mortal mind cannot readily accept this idea. Few Christian thinkers (certainly not Milton) would say that the sin of Adam and Eve was an unequivocally good thing. Rather, the fall and the resurrection are both intimate parts of God's providence—he foresees them both and sees them outside of time, existing together. Humankind, on the other hand, must do its best in a temporal world, dealing with the decisions of the present. As Adam and Eve leave Paradise, they know that obedience to God and love for his creation can help humankind toward its salvation, and lead humankind toward regaining the Paradise that has been lost.

Important Quotations Explained

1. Of Man's First Disobedience, and the Fruit
    Of that Forbidden Tree, whose mortal taste
    Brought Death into the World, and all our woe,
    With loss of Eden, till one greater Man
    Restore us, and regain the blissful
    Seat, Sing Heav'nly Muse, that on the secret top
    Of Oreb, or of Sinai, didst inspire
    That Shepherd, who first taught the chosen
    Seed, In the Beginning how the Heav'ns and Earth
    Rose out of Chaos: Or if Sion Hill
    Delight thee more, and Siloa's Brook that flow'd
    Fast by the Oracle of God; I thence
    Invoke thy aid to my advent'rous Song,
    That with no middle flight intends to soar
    Above th' Aonian Mount, while it pursues
    Things unattempted yet in Prose or Rhyme.
        (I.1–26)

With these lines, Milton begins *Paradise Lost* and lays the groundwork for his project, presenting his purpose, subject, aspirations, and need for heavenly guidance. He states that his subject will be the disobedience of Adam and Eve, whose sin allows death and pain into the world. He invokes his muse, whom he identifies as the Holy Spirit. He asserts his hopes that his epic poem will surpass the other great epic poems written before, as he claims that his story is the most original and the most virtuous. He also asks his muse to fill his mind with divine knowledge so that he can share this knowledge with his readers. Finally, he hopes this knowledge and guidance from his muse will allow him to claim authority without committing any heresies, as he attempts to explain God's reasoning and his overall plan for humankind.

2.   Hail holy Light, offspring of Heav'n first-born,
      Or of th' Eternal Coeternal beam
      May I express thee unblam'd? since God is Light,
      And never but in unapproached Light
      Dwelt from Eternity, dwelt then in thee,
      Bright effluence of bright essence increate.

      . . .

      thee I revisit safe,
      And feel thy Sovran vital Lamp; but thou
      Revisit'st not these eyes, that roll in vain
      To find thy piercing ray, and find no dawn;
      So thick a drop serene hath quencht thir Orbs,
      Or dim suffusion veil'd. Yet not the more
      Cease I to wander where the Muses haunt
      Clear Spring, or shady Grove, or Sunny Hill,
      Smit with the love of sacred Song . . .

      . . .

      So much the rather thou Celestial Light
      Shine inward, and the mind through all powers
      Irradiate, there plant eyes, all mist from thence
      Purge and disperse, that I may see and tell
      Of things invisible to mortal sight.
         (III.1–6; 21–29; 51–55)

These passages from Book III make up part of Milton's second and longest invocation, which is also his most autobiographical and symbolic. Milton refers to light simultaneously as divine wisdom and literal light. When he speaks about his blindness he refers to both his inward blindness, or lack of divine wisdom, and his literal blindness, or loss of eyesight.

He begins by praising holy light as the essence of God. The idea that God is light was common before and during Milton's time, and is a popular interpretation of certain biblical passages in Genesis. He then invokes his heavenly muse, the Holy Spirit, by reusing similar images and ideas from his first invocation; remember that Milton has asked for this heaven muse to illuminate "what in me is dark" (I.22). Symbolically, Milton asks for his muse to enter his body and fill him with divine knowledge.

Milton discusses his physical, outward blindness when he compares himself to other famous blind "Prophets old" (III.36), such as Homer (Maeonides) and Tiresias, and asks that he be filled with even more wisdom than them. He does not seek pity for his blindness, explaining that he is still active and undeterred from his poetic purpose. He believes that his outward blindness is insignificant, and that he hopes he is not inwardly blind. He hopes to sing beautifully like the darkling bird, which sings at night, unable to see who or what she is singing to. He ends his invocation by asking for his inward blindness to be corrected so that he can properly tell the story of Adam and Eve.

3.   . . . though both
        Not equal, as thir sex not equal seem'd;
        For contemplation hee and valor form'd,
        For softness shee and sweet attractive Grace,
        Hee for God only, shee for God in him:
        His fair large Front and Eye sublime declar'd
        Absolute rule; and Hyacinthine Locks
        Round from his parted forelock manly hung
        Clust'ring, but not beneath his shoulders broad:
        Shee as a veil down to the slender waist
        Her unadorned golden tresses wore
        Dishevell'd, but in wanton ringlets wav'd
        As the Vine curls her tendrils, which impli'd
        Subjection, but requir'd with gentle sway,
        And by her yielded, by him best receiv'd,
        Yielded with coy submission, modest pride,
        And sweet reluctant amorous delay.
        (IV.295–311)

The narrator makes these observations in Book IV as Adam and Eve prepare for bed. The narrator compares Adam and Eve based on their appearance and general demeanor, reasoning from that in order to assess their spiritual value. The argument behind the description lies in their different roles: since Adam was created for God, and Eve was created for both God and Adam, Eve's purpose makes her less spiritually pure and farther removed from God's grace. She serves both God and Adam and submits to Adam out of love and duty to God. He notes that Adam seems to be more intelligent and spiritually pure than Eve.

This assessment illustrates Milton's belief that male and female genders and their roles are unequal. The Bible also speaks of these unequal roles, arguing that a wife should submit and serve her husband. These beliefs were common in Milton's time, as many people believed they were sanctioned by the Bible. This apparent gender imbalance between Adam and Eve is continually portrayed throughout the rest of *Paradise Lost*.

4. What better can we do, than to place
  Repairing where he judg'd us, prostrate fall
  Before him reverent, and there confess
  Humbly our faults, and pardon beg, with tears
  Watering the ground, and with our sighs the
  Air Frequenting, sent from hearts contrite, in sigh
  Of sorrow unfeign'd, and humiliation meek.
  Undoubtedly he will relent and turn
  From his displeasure; in whose look serene,
  When angry most he seem'd and most severe,
  What else but favor, grace, and mercy shone?
  So spake our Father penitent, nor Eve
  Felt less remorse: they forthwith to the place
  Repairing where he judg'd them prostrate fell
  Before him reverent, and both confess'd
  Humbly their faults, and pardon begg'd, with tears
  Watering the ground, and with their sighs the
  Air Frequenting, sent from hearts contrite, in sign
  Of sorrow unfeign'd, and humiliation meek.
  (X.1086–1104)

These lines at the end of Book X, first spoken by Adam, and then narrated by Milton, relate Adam and Eve's decision to pray to God for forgiveness and their subsequent action of prayer. This point in the story finds Adam and Eve choosing between obedience and disobedience. Their repentance allows them to be forgiven, and their forgiveness allows for the possible redemption of humankind. These lines present the first step in humankind's long search for salvation.

 Much of Adam's speech and Milton's narration overlaps; many lines are repeated with only the tenses and pronouns changed. This use of repetition has a dramatic effect on a dramatic and important scene. Milton's use of repetition gives his narration an emotional accuracy and compassionate tone. And the repetition places extra emphasis on their act of prayer, allowing readers to understand its extreme importance to the story. It also demonstrates that Adam and Eve repent exactly what they planned in the way they planned it, showing their dedication and determination to obey God strictly even after the fall.

5.   This having learnt, thou hast attained the sum
      Of Wisdom; hope no higher, though all the Stars
      Thou knew'st by name, and all th' ethereal Powers,
      All secrets of the deep, all Nature's works,
      Or works of God in Heav'n, Air, Earth, or Sea,
      And all riches of this World enjoy'dst,
      And all the rule, one Empire: only add
      Deeds to thy knowledge answerable, add Faith,
      Add Virtue, Patience, Temperance, add Love,
      By name to come called Charity, the soul
      Of all the rest: then wilt though not be loth
      To leave this Paradise, but shalt possess
      A paradise within thee, happier far.
          (XII.575–587)

These lines are spoken by Michael to Adam in Book XII just before Adam and Eve are led out of Paradise. Michael tries to explain to Adam that even though Eve and him have fallen from grace and must leave Paradise, they can still lead a fruitful life. He tells Adam that he has attained all the wisdom he needs; any further knowledge is unnecessary. To assure their happiness, they should live their lives by seven tenets: obedience, faith, virtue, patience, temperance, love, and charity. Living by these tenets will allow them to create an inner Paradise. In contrast, the seven sins allow Satan to create his inner Hell, which he discusses in Book IV. Even though Satan is in Paradise, he feels as if he is still in Hell. Likewise, Adam and Eve can feel as if they never left Paradise if they live their lives accordingly. Heaven and Hell become more than just a place, they become a state of mind.

QUOTATIONS

KEY FACTS

KEY FACTS

FULL TITLE
  Paradise Lost

AUTHOR
  John Milton

TYPE OF WORK
  Poem

GENRE
  Epic

LANGUAGE
  English

TIME AND PLACE WRITTEN
  1656–1674; England

DATE OF FIRST PUBLICATION
  First Edition (ten books), 1667; Second Edition (twelve books),
  1674

PUBLISHER
  S. Simmons, England

NARRATOR
  Milton

POINT OF VIEW
  Third person

TONE
  Lofty; formal; tragic

TENSE
  Present

SETTING (TIME)
  Before the beginning of time

SETTING (PLACE)
  Hell, Chaos and Night, Heaven, Earth (Paradise, the Garden
  of Eden)

PROTAGONIST
   Adam and Eve

MAJOR CONFLICT
   Satan, already damned to Hell, undertakes to corrupt God's new,
   beloved creation, humankind.

RISING ACTION
   The angels battle in Heaven; Satan and the rebel angels fall to
   Hell; God creates the universe; Satan plots to corrupt God's
   human creation; God creates Eve to be Adam's companion;
   Raphael answers Adam's questions and warns him of Satan

CLIMAX
   Adam and Eve eat the fruit of the Tree of Knowledge.

FALLING ACTION
   The Son inflicts punishment; Adam and Eve repent; Adam learns
   about the future of man

THEMES
   The Importance of Obedience to God; The Hierarchical Nature
   of the Universe; The Fall as Partly Fortunate

MOTIFS
   Light and Dark; The Geography of the Universe; Conversation
   and Contemplation

SYMBOLS
   The Scales in the Sky; Adam's wreath

FORESHADOWING
   Eve's vanity at seeing her reflection in the lake; Satan's
   transformation into a snake and his final punishment

KEY FACTS

STUDY QUESTIONS & ESSAY TOPICS

STUDY QUESTIONS

1. *Satan is the most well-developed character in Paradise Lost. Is he a sympathetic character? Examine one of his soliloquies and identify the character traits and poetic techniques that make him seem appealing or forgivable.*

One reason that Satan is easy to sympathize with is that he is much more like us than God or the Son are. As the embodiment of human errors, he is much easier for us to imagine and empathize with than an omniscient deity. Satan's character and psychology are all very human, and his envy, pride, and despair are understandable given his situation. But Satan's speeches, while undeniably moving, subtly display their own inconsistency and error.

When Satan first sees Earth and Paradise in Book III, he is overcome with grief. His description of his situation is eloquent; his expression of pain is moving. Perhaps we pity Satan as he struggles to find his new identity while reflecting on his recent mistakes. Likewise, his feeling of despair resonates with feelings that all human beings undergo at some point. However, Satan's despair becomes fuel for his ever-increasing evil, rather than the foundation for repentance. His anger and irrationality overcomes him, and he resolves to make evil his virtue. In many ways Satan becomes more understandable in this speech for his pitiable human qualities, and he becomes more interesting as well due to the unpredictability of his character. But overall, his ever-increasing stubbornness and devilish pride makes him less forgivable.

2. *Trace the appearance of autobiographical details in Paradise Lost. How are these details important to the story? What is the identity and role of the narrator?*

Traditionally, critics make a distinction between the author and the speaker of a poem, or between the author and the narrator. *Paradise Lost,* however, identifies the narrator with Milton in several of the invocations that open individual books. Milton inserts autobiographical references to make the reader know that it is he—not an imaginary, unnamed character—who is narrating.

The autobiographical details in Milton's three invocations allow Milton to simultaneously express his purpose and his Christian humility. Milton explains to his audience that his purpose is just and his humility is real. First, in his invocation in Book I, he hopes his darkness (or blindness) will be illuminated so he can learn the facts of his story he will tell. In his second invocation, in Book III, he praises Holy Light and again hopes that his blindness will be corrected, at least metaphorically. He also expresses his fear that he may have waited too long to begin writing his epic poem; he fears his age may cloud his reason, or that he has passed his creative and stylistic peaks. In the final invocation, in Book VII, Milton asks for help in making the narrative transition from Heaven to Earth. In a display of humility, he asks for help in finishing his story. This invocation presents Milton as a devoted follower and writer with fallible qualities. His pleas to his heavenly muse parallel Adam and Eve's repentance and request for guidance. Milton's interjections diminish the possibility that the story will become simply a vehicle of his ego and opinions. These autobiographical details endow his narration with a sense of authority.

QUESTIONS & ESSAYS

3. *Traditional Christian belief holds that the Son and the
   Father are two parts of the same God, but Milton
   presents the Son as a fundamentally separate entity
   from God the Father. How does this distinction affect
   the plot of Paradise Lost?*

Milton deviates from traditional Christian theology concerning the
Holy Trinity. He explains in *Paradise Lost* his belief that God the
Father existed with the Holy Spirit, another part of the Trinity, who
wandered about the "vast abyss" (I.21). But, Milton explains, God
the Son had not yet been created. God the Father creates him afterward, and appoints him as his second-in-command. Indeed, this
depiction of the Son's origin conflicts with the Bible. But in both the
Bible and in Milton's story, the appointment of the Son as second-in-
command leads to Satan's envy and rebellion. In this way, Milton's
separation of the Father and the Son allows for Satan's outrage to be
more understandable, and at least more believable. While Milton
did not completely believe in every aspect of the Holy Trinity as it
was believed by others in his time, he does believe that God the
Father and God the Son have equal powers but with different roles.

The Father and the Son are essentially one entity, but the con-
struction of *Paradise Lost* as a story with characters who must inter-
act with each other allows Milton to explore their separate roles and
their unfathomable relationship. In many scenes, God the Father
sends God the Son to perform certain tasks, like the creation of the
universe, of Earth, and Adam. The Bible explains that God himself,
not Jesus the Son, performed these tasks, and Milton agrees. In these
scenes, the Father merely works through his Son. Since Milton
believes that God the Father is unknowable and unimaginable, God
the Son becomes his knowable and imaginable representation. In
other words, the Son (Jesus) becomes the mobile version of God and
the mediator between humankind and God the Father.

Suggested Essay Topics

1. *Milton places great emphasis on man's autonomous reason and free will. Do Adam and Eve show evidence of being ruled by reason before the fall?*

2. *Examine the passages in which Milton discusses the nature of women as compared to men. Do you think it is correct to label Milton a misogynist?*

3. Paradise Lost *includes many characters who can be easily compared and contrasted with each other. For instance, God and Satan stand as complete opposites; Satan, Sin, and Death form an evil version of the Holy Trinity; Adam and Eve seem to be far from equally made and disposed for life in Paradise; even God the Father and God the Son have differences. Pick one of these pairs and describe their differences as well as their similarities.*

4. *Based on the text of* Paradise Lost, *how do you think Milton would justify his alterations of and additions to the Bible, given the fact that he was a devout Christian?*

QUESTIONS & ESSAYS

REVIEW & RESOURCES

QUIZ

1. Which angel does Satan trick by disguising himself as a cherub?

    A.   Michael
    B.   Uriel
    C.   Raphael
    D.   Abdiel

2. Which of the following forms does Satan not take?

    A.   Angel
    B.   Toad
    C.   Cormorant
    D.   He takes all of these forms

3. In what book does the fall take place?

    A.   Book VIII
    B.   Book X
    C.   Book IX
    D.   Book VII

4. In which book of the Bible does the story of Adam and Eve occur?

    A.   Leviticus
    B.   Exodus
    C.   Genesis
    D.   Deuteronomy

5. Which devil advocates a renewal of all-out war against God?

    A.   Belial
    B.   Moloch
    C.   Mammon
    D.   Beelzebub

6. What is Milton's stated purpose in Paradise Lost?

   A. To assert his superiority to other poets
   B. To argue against the doctrine of predestination
   C. To justify the ways of God to men
   D. To make his story hard to understand

7. Which of the following is not a character in Paradise Lost?

   A. Night
   B. Agony
   C. Discord
   D. Death

8. Which angel wields a large sword in the battle and wounds Satan?

   A. Michael
   B. Abdiel
   C. Uriel
   D. Satan is not injured

9. When Satan leaps over the fence into Paradise, what does Milton liken him to?

   A. A snake slithering up a tree
   B. A germ infecting a body
   C. A wolf leaping into a sheep's pen
   D. A fish leaping out of water

10. Which angel tells Adam about the future in Books XI and XII?

    A. Raphael
    B. Uriel
    C. Michael
    D. None of the above

11. Which of the following is not found in Hell?

    A. Gems
    B. Gold
    C. Oil
    D. Minerals

12. Which statement about the Earth is asserted as true in Paradise Lost?

    A. It was created before God the Son
    B. Earth hangs from Heaven by a chain
    C. The Earth is a lotus flower
    D. The Earth revolves around the sun

13. Which devil is the main architect of Pandemonium?

    A. Mulciber
    B. Mammon
    C. Moloch
    D. Belial

14. How many times does Milton invoke a muse?

    A. One
    B. Two
    C. Three
    D. Four

15. Who leads Adam and Eve out of Paradise?

    A. God
    B. The Son
    C. Michael
    D. Raphael

16. Which of the following poets does Milton emulate?

    A. Virgil
    B. Homer
    C. Both Virgil and Homer
    D. Neither Virgil or Homer

17. What is the stated subject of Paradise Lost?

    A. The fight between good and evil
    B. Heaven's battle and Satan's tragic fall
    C. The creation of the universe
    D. Adam and Eve's disobedience

REVIEW & RESOURCES

18. Which devil is Satan's second-in-command?

    A.   Mammon
    B.   Sin
    C.   Moloch
    D.   Beezlebub

19. Who discusses cosmology and the battle of Heaven with Adam?

    A.   God
    B.   Eve
    C.   Raphael
    D.   Michael

20. Which scene happens first chronologically?

    A.   Satan and the devils rise up from the lake in Hell
    B.   The Son is chosen as God's second-in-command
    C.   God and the Son create the universe
    D.   The angels battle in Heaven

21. Which of the angels is considered a hero for arguing against Satan?

    A.   Abdiel
    B.   Uriel
    C.   Michael
    D.   Raphael

22. In an attempt to defeat God and his angels, what do the rebel angels make?

    A.   A fortress
    B.   A catapult
    C.   A large sword
    D.   A cannon

23. According to Paradise Lost, which of the following does God not create?

   A. The Son
   B. Adam and Eve
   C. Computers
   D. He creates everything

24. Who does Milton name as his heavenly muse?

   A. Titania
   B. Urania
   C. Virgil
   D. Michael

25. What does Eve do when she first becomes conscious?

   A. Go in search of her mate
   B. Talk to the animals
   C. Look at her reflection in a stream
   D. Eat of the Tree of Knowledge

ANSWER KEY:

1: B; 2: D; 3: C; 4: C; 5: B; 6: C; 7: B; 8: A; 9: C; 10: C;
11: C; 12: B; 13: A; 14: C; 15: C; 16: C; 17: D; 18: D; 19: C;
20: B; 21: A; 22: D; 23: D; 24: B; 25: C

Suggestions for Further Reading

ELLEDGE, SCOTT. "Introduction to *Paradise Lost*." In PARADISE LOST. W.W. Norton, 1975: xi–xxix.

EVANS, J. MARTIN. *Milton's Imperial Epic: PARADISE LOST and the Discourse of Colonialism*. Ithaca, NY: Cornell University Press, 1996.

FISH, STANLEY. *Surprised by Sin: The Reader in PARADISE LOST*. Cambridge: Harvard University Press, 1967.

LEWIS, C.S. *A Preface to PARADISE LOST*. New York: Oxford University Press, 1961.

PARKER, WILLIAM RILEY. *Milton: A Biography*. New York: Oxford University Press, 1968.

LEWALSKI, BARBARA KIEFER. PARADISE LOST *and the Rhetoric of Literary Forms*. Princeton, NJ: Princeton University Press, 1985.

RAJAN, BALACHANDRA. PARADISE LOST *and the Seventeenth Century Reader*. Ann Arbor, MI: University of Michigan Press, 1967.

SHAWCROSS, JOHN T. *John Milton: The Self and the World*. Lexington, KY: University Press of Kentucky, 1993.

SHAWCROSS, JOHN T. *With Mortal Voice: The Creation of PARADISE LOST*. Lexington, KY: University Press of Kentucky, 1982.

WALKER, JULIA M., ed. *Milton and the Idea of Woman*. Urbana, IL: University of Illinois Press, 1988.

WHEELER, THOMAS. PARADISE LOST *and the Modern Reader*. Athens, GA: University of Georgia Press, 1974.

ZUNDER, WILLIAM, ed. PARADISE LOST: *John Milton*. New York: St. Martin's Press, 1999.

REVIEW & RESOURCES

SparkNotes™ Literature Guides

1984
The Adventures of
  Huckleberry Finn
The Adventures of Tom
  Sawyer
The Aeneid
All Quiet on the
  Western Front
And Then There Were
  None
Angela's Ashes
Animal Farm
Anna Karenina
Anne of Green Gables
Anthem
Antony and Cleopatra
Aristotle's Ethics
As I Lay Dying
As You Like It
Atlas Shrugged
The Awakening
The Autobiography of
  Malcolm X
The Bean Trees
The Bell Jar
Beloved
Beowulf
Billy Budd
Black Boy
Bless Me, Ultima
The Bluest Eye
Brave New World
The Brothers
  Karamazov
The Call of the Wild
Candide
The Canterbury Tales
Catch-22
The Catcher in the Rye
The Chocolate War
The Chosen
Cold Mountain
Cold Sassy Tree
The Color Purple
The Count of Monte
  Cristo
Crime and Punishment
The Crucible
Cry, the Beloved
  Country
Cyrano de Bergerac
David Copperfield

Death of a Salesman
The Death of Socrates
The Diary of a Young
  Girl
A Doll's House
Don Quixote
Dr. Faustus
Dr. Jekyll and Mr. Hyde
Dracula
Dune
East of Eden
Edith Hamilton's
  Mythology
Emma
Ethan Frome
Fahrenheit 451
Fallen Angels
A Farewell to Arms
Farewell to Manzanar
Flowers for Algernon
For Whom the Bell
  Tolls
The Fountainhead
Frankenstein
The Giver
The Glass Menagerie
Gone With the Wind
The Good Earth
The Grapes of Wrath
Great Expectations
The Great Gatsby
Greek Classics
Grendel
Gulliver's Travels
Hamlet
The Handmaid's Tale
Hard Times
Harry Potter and the
  Sorcerer's Stone
Heart of Darkness
Henry IV, Part I
Henry V
Hiroshima
The Hobbit
The House of Seven
  Gables
I Know Why the Caged
  Bird Sings
The Iliad
Inferno
Inherit the Wind
Invisible Man

Jane Eyre
Johnny Tremain
The Joy Luck Club
Julius Caesar
The Jungle
The Killer Angels
King Lear
The Last of the
  Mohicans
Les Miserables
A Lesson Before Dying
The Little Prince
Little Women
Lord of the Flies
The Lord of the Rings
Macbeth
Madame Bovary
A Man for All Seasons
The Mayor of
  Casterbridge
The Merchant of Venice
A Midsummer Night's
  Dream
Moby Dick
Much Ado About
  Nothing
My Antonia
Narrative of the Life of
  Frederick Douglass
Native Son
The New Testament
Night
Notes from
  Underground
The Odyssey
The Oedipus Plays
Of Mice and Men
The Old Man and the
  Sea
The Old Testament
Oliver Twist
The Once and Future
  King
One Day in the Life of
  Ivan Denisovich
One Flew Over the
  Cuckoo's Nest
One Hundred Years of
  Solitude
Othello
Our Town
The Outsiders

Paradise Lost
A Passage to India
The Pearl
The Picture of Dorian
  Gray
Poe's Short Stories
A Portrait of the Artist
  as a Young Man
Pride and Prejudice
The Prince
A Raisin in the Sun
The Red Badge of
  Courage
The Republic
Richard III
Robinson Crusoe
Romeo and Juliet
The Scarlet Letter
A Separate Peace
Silas Marner
Sir Gawain and the
  Green Knight
Slaughterhouse-Five
Snow Falling on Cedars
Song of Solomon
The Sound and the Fury
Steppenwolf
The Stranger
Streetcar Named
  Desire
The Sun Also Rises
A Tale of Two Cities
The Taming of the
  Shrew
The Tempest
Tess of the d'Ubervilles
Their Eyes Were
  Watching God
Things Fall Apart
The Things They
  Carried
To Kill a Mockingbird
To the Lighthouse
Treasure Island
Twelfth Night
Ulysses
Uncle Tom's Cabin
Walden
War and Peace
Wuthering Heights
A Yellow Raft in Blue
  Water